SEPECAT
JAGUAR

SEPECAT JAGUAR

ALMOST EXTINCT

PETER FOSTER

The History Press

First published 2017

The History Press
The Mill, Brimscombe Port
Stroud, Gloucestershire, GL5 2QG
www.thehistorypress.co.uk

British Library Cataloguing in Publication Data.
A catalogue record for this book is available from the British
Library.

ISBN 978 0 07509 7021 1

Typesetting and origination by The History Press
Printed and bound in India by Replika Press Pvt. Ltd.

Front cover: RAFO jet 210 over the Dofar region of Oman on a sortie
from Thumrait in February 2009. (Author's collection)

Back cover: GR 3A XX725 at RAF Coningsby on the day of the
squadron's disbandment in 2007. (Author's collection)

CONTENTS

A Simon Watson photograph of an Indian Air Force Maritime Strike Jaguar. The Jaguar IM were the first to incorporate the DARIN III avionics upgrade.

PREFACE

THE DECISION TO PRODUCE a sequel to the highly successful book *Sepecat Jaguar: Endangered Species* was born out of the continuing interest in the type and my own personal need to see some near closure on the history of this remarkable aeroplane. The timing of publication is poignant and coincides with the 10th anniversary of the type's retirement from the RAF. This has enabled me to bring together my previous research into one complete book. For the sake of reference I have retained some historical information, suitably updated, from the previous book.

Since I wrote the first book five of the six countries to have operated the Jaguar have retired the jet. Only India continues to operate the aircraft, and through a series of significant upgrades will in all probability continue in service for another decade.

In the UK the Jaguar's last hurrah came with almost indecent haste, as the retirement date was brought forward with little thought to the crews and personnel involved in its operation or the vacuum that its departure would leave behind. Alas, recent history on the management of RAF front-line assets

has seen such history repeated all in the name of reduced defence spending.

Of the Jaguar's overseas partners Nigeria ultimately put its surviving airframes up for sale without ever returning them to service, although there were apparently no takers. Ecuador held its Jaguar force in warm storage for the best part of a decade before it too decided it was time to draw a line under its operation. Only Oman succeeded in keeping the Jaguar in front-line service beyond its original retirement date although it too had to bow down to age and the final flight took place on 6 August 2014.

India on the other hand was still producing the Jaguar right up to 2010 and currently plans to keep the aircraft at the front of its offensive thinking for at least another decade. The upgrades already incorporated and those currently proposed will ensure that the claws of the Jaguar will remain as sharp as ever.

Peter R. Foster
Doddington, Cambs
May 2017

In the final weeks of front-line operation the Jaguar force by now 'down declared' to NATO went back to what it did best – low-level operation. In this shot 'EB' of No. 6 Squadron is seen passing through the Machynlleth Loop in mid Wales.

ROYAL AIR FORCE FAREWELL – THE FINAL DAYS

THE OFFICER COMMANDING No. 6 Squadron, Wing Commander John Sullivan, wrote on the website PPRuNe on 24 April 2007:

Today I announced to the members of 6 Squadron that the Jaguar OSD is to be brought forward to 30 April 07. All operationally oriented training will cease on this date and the Jaguar will no longer be a deployable Force Element. Delivery of the airframes to Cosford will then commence and I have been instructed that any ceremonial flying must be concluded during May.

So came the abrupt end to the RAF Jaguar operation. However, it is perhaps appropriate to look back at that final year of operations since the closure of RAF Coltishall (the Jaguar's spiritual home), the relocation of No. 6 Squadron and the demise of No. 41 Squadron at that time.

Less than two years previously, Flight Lieutenant Matt D'Aubyn graduated in the RAF and was to be its last ever Jaguar pilot when he passed through the doors of No. 41 Squadron Jaguar Training Flight on 10 October 2005 to his operational posting with No. 6 Squadron. No. 16 Squadron had the previous role of front-line Jaguar training and it had succumbed to the inevitable only six months earlier allowing the small output now required to be handled by a separate flight of No. 41 Squadron.

Matt D'Aubyn was a classic product of RAF fast jet training – a sharp, well-focused individual that the RAF produces on a regular basis. His short eighteen months on the venerable Jaguar will no doubt have stood him in good stead for his future opportunities. Since the Jaguar entered service the RAF had

Opposite: Wing Commander John Sullivan leads the farewell fly-past over XX725 towards the reviewing officer and disbandment parade.

Above: Royal Air Force Coltishall.

Right: Air Commodore Graham Wright brings the parade to attention at the RAF Coltishall disbandment ceremony.

trained 1,038 students, of which 841 were new pilots converting onto the aircraft for the first time. Prior to the first course at RAF Lossiemouth in May 1973, a number of pilots were trained to fly the aircraft by the manufacturer. The RAF had also trained pilots from overseas, including those from countries that had acquired the Jaguar like Oman, Ecuador, Nigeria and India. They also trained several pilots on exchange tours such as those from Germany, United States and New Zealand.

RAF Coltishall itself had closed its doors to operational flying on 1 April 2006 when the station commander, Air Commodore Graham Wright, led the final formation fly-past before heading off to the Jaguar's new home at RAF Coningsby.

In typical April weather, the fly-past comprised of Jaguar T.Mk 4s XX835/EX, XX847/EZ and GR.3As XZ103/FP, XZ117/FB and XZ391/ET. There had been a sixth aircraft, XZ112/GW, but this had reportedly

Sepecat Jaguar GR.3A XZ103 sporting the No. 41 Squadron anniversary colour scheme at the disbandment ceremony.

incurred a last-minute technical malfunction and had aborted. It was suggested at the time that this was pre-planned to ensure that the final aircraft to leave Coltishall was a Jaguar, so as not to be upstaged in history by any of the visiting aircraft that had been prepositioned for this final day!

The remainder of the aircraft that had up until 31 March been assigned to the two RAF Coltishall squadrons had departed for their new home a couple of days earlier on 29 March. They, however, returned on 1 April for a nine-ship diamond formation fly-past with call signs 'Boxer 1–9'. Two others, XZ399/EJ and XX752/EK, had acted as air spares with call signs 'Boxer 10–11'.

The nine-ship formation comprised of all single-seat Jaguar GR.3As: XX723/FF, XX725/FE, XX738/ED, XX748/EG, XX767/FK, XZ109/EN, XZ114/EO, XZ115/ER and XZ392/EM.

At an interview held at the demise of the Jaguar, Wing Commander John Sullivan, who had led this formation, recalled that on the run into Coltishall, air traffic advised him that the reviewing officer – Air Chief Marshal Sir Jock Stirrup, Chief of the Air Staff (CAS) and a former Jaguar pilot – was running late and to delay the fly-past! Sullivan then had to reverse the formation, which was no mean feat, on being ordered to 'spin cold', only to be advised halfway around the turn that the reviewing officer was now ready and to 'spin hot'! Needless to say the formation duly arrived at the appointed moment.

RAF Coltishall itself finally closed its doors as an RAF station on 30 November 2006.

For the squadron at RAF Coningsby the next year was certainly a busy one. 21 April 2006 saw ten aircraft deploy to Oman on Exercise Magic Carpet followed by taking part in the Queen's birthday fly-past. In September of the same year ten aircraft undertook a similar exercise in Jordan maintaining their 'Flying Canopeners' links with the Middle East.

Above: Wing Commander John Sullivan leading the 'Diamond Nine' overhead the disbandment 'salute' at RAF Coltishall.

Above right: Line-up of Jaguar tails on the final day of flying at RAF Coltishall showing the No. 41 Squadron anniversary marks, the No. 6 squadron 'Flying Canopeners' strip and the RAF Coltishall station anniversary jet.

Then on 11 March 2007 seven aircraft set off for Al Dhafra on what was believed to have been exercise Iron Falcon. It was whilst on this exercise that the decision to bring forward the Jaguar OSD was made public. This was a surprising move considering the fact that it was in the public domain before the squadron had been officially told.

Five of the jets – XX112/EA, XX738/ED, XX748/EG, XZ398/EQ and XZ399/EJ – returned to Coningsby on 14 April followed on 25 April by the remaining two – XX752/EK and XX970/EH. It was on this day that Wing Commander John Sullivan had to officially tell his troops of the decision to bring forward the Jaguar OSD.

It is best left to the words of Squadron Leader Dheeraj Bhasin in an article he wrote for *RAF News* to sum up that final month before the official disbandment took place:

The Squadron, which was rapidly diminishing in size due to personnel being re-assigned, set about preparing the squadron infrastructure for handover to No XI Squadron, the second operational Typhoon squadron, which was to take over the site. This involved removal of Jaguar-specific equipment from the Hardened Aircraft Shelters and technical accommodation, and, of course, removal of the 6 Squadron

memorabilia and markings. Much of the Squadron's memorabilia is of historic value – it is the longest continuously serving air force squadron in the world – and has to be preserved for when the Squadron reforms as a Typhoon squadron. As a final tribute to the aircraft (and so that no one forgets the 'cat') some 'decorations' were left behind, which can be seen on a couple of shelters – lest we forget!

It had been envisaged that the No. 6 Squadron lineage would have continued unbroken into a seamless Typhoon transition, but with ever tightening budgets this was not to be.

Although operational flying had ceased, pilot currency had to be maintained for both the planned farewell fly-past and delivery of the aircraft to RAF Cosford. This saw a fair amount of general handling sorties that in themselves provided opportunities for the Jaguar to be seen in its true environment – 'down in the weeds'.

A number of farewell fly-pasts took place during that month, with the final disbandment event occurring on 31 May 2007. Wing Commander John Sullivan led a seven-ship formation comprising two Jaguar T.4 aircraft and five GR.3As arriving overhead of the reviewing officer and RAF band on the main Coningsby ASP at the appropriate moment of

Air Commodore Graham Wright with Squadron Leader Ian Smith crewing in for the final fly-past at RAF Coltishall.

Above: Air Commodore Graham Wright in Jaguar T.4 XX835 leads the final fly-past over the parade as the reviewing officer takes the salute.

Above right: Air Chief Marshal Sir Jock Stirrup, Chief of the Air Staff, inspecting the parade at RAF Coltishall prior to taking the farewell salute.

the salute. This was set against the background of two of the squadron's aircraft, XX112/EA and XX725/T, the latter resplendent in the desert-pink scheme of the Gulf War in which the squadron had acquitted itself so well.

All that was now left was for the squadron's sixteen aircraft to be ferried to their final destinations. Five aircraft departed Coningsby on 18 May for RAF Cosford comprising XX729, XX738, XX748, XX847 and XZ398. These were followed on 13 June by eight more: XX112, XX724, XX752, XX840, XX970, XZ103, XZ392 and XZ399. The large gap between deliveries was dictated on weather factors as the runway at RAF Cosford was reasonably short and lacked appropriate equipment for fast jet operation. The crews needed a dry runway and appropriate wind speeds.

The final three aircraft, XX119, XX725 and XX835, departed Coningsby on 2 July crewed by Wing Commander John Sullivan OBE and Squadron Leader Ian Smith, with Mark Hodge (the senior engineering officer) in the back seat, and Flight Lieutenant Mark D'Aubyn (the youngest pilot on the squadron and the last RAF Jaguar pilot to be trained). This brought to an end the RAF Jaguar operation.

Jaguar's Last Hurrah

Although the Jaguar had officially ceased to be an operational asset within the annals of the RAF, QinetiQ at Boscombe Down still held two aircraft: Jaguar GR.3A XZ117 that No. 6 Squadron had delivered in the final days and Jaguar T.Mk

The pilots of the final fly-past line-up with Air Commodore Graham Wright, third from left, for a nostalgic farewell picture against the backdrop of Jaguar GR.3A XZ112.

The final chapter in RAF operation of the venerable Sepecat Jaguar saw No. 6 Squadron undertake a number of high-profile events, beginning with the 2006 Queen's birthday fly-past. Here XX723 is seen in close formation during the practice event on 14 June.

2A(T) XX833. The former was believed to have been received to provide a ready on-site source of spares, whilst the latter was still very much alive and well and used both by the Empire Test Pilots School (ETPS) and the QinetiQ Fast Jet Test Squadrons test pilots.

The aircraft had been on MoD strength for a number of years in use with 'A' Flight RAE at Farnborough from 1989, Central Trials & Test Organisation (CTTO) at Boscombe Down in 1994, the DRA Experimental Flying Squadron and eventually QinetiQ as part of the Aircraft Test and Evaluation Centre (ATEC) operation in July 2001.

One of its last major trials was that of the Thermal Imaging Airborne Laser Designation (TIALD) research aircraft. Named 'Night Cat' it was variously described as being both a Jaguar T.Mk 2B and T.Mk 2A(T), whilst QinetiQ itself referred to the jet as a plain T.2A. However, the jet had been used as a development test vehicle for the Jaguar 1996–97 updates and had a number of systems broadly comparable with those fitted to the T.Mk 4 aircraft.

Whilst on strength of the test organisations the jet had received a comprehensive instrumentation makeover. The addition of recording and telemetry systems and the removal of the Aden gun facility coupled with modification of the ammunition tanks to accommodate its experimental fits.

A Head Tracker System (HTS) had been fitted to give steering and target information to the Navigation and Weapon Aiming Sub-System (NAVWASS). The HTS was used in conjunction with HMD (Helmet Mounted Display), Display NVG (Night Vision Goggles), or Integrated Panoramic NVG (IPNVG) to provide a Helmet Mounted Sight (HMS) facility.

However, its life beyond RAF Jaguar was limited; as its airframe life began to run out of hours it too was headed for retirement.

Its last flight took place on 20 December 2007. Piloted by Squadron Leader Andy Blythe and accompanied by Wing Commander Paul Shakespeare (both from Fast Jet Squadron, based at MoD Boscombe Down) it took off at around 11.30 a.m. The jet undertook a medium-level flight routing

The Queen's birthday fly-past practice used on this occasion RAF Waddington as the datum. Here XX723 is seen from the lead RAF VC.10K3 ZA148 as the formation turns over Bracebridge Heath, with the old Lancaster production hangars clearly visible below.

Jaguar GR.3A XZ117 was part of the four-ship Queen's birthday fly-past seen over the Lincolnshire countryside. This aircraft was flown initially to Boscombe Down upon retirement to serve as a spares source for the QinetiQ XX833.

via RAF Coltishall, RAF Coningsby and BAE Systems Warton – all locations with a long Jaguar heritage. It also overflew RAF Marham, where a number of former Jaguar engineers were then based, before recovering into Boscombe Down.

Its very last flight took place in the afternoon at around 3.00 p.m. This was a low-level sortie around Wales prior to an overflight of St Athan and a final return to Boscombe Down, touching down at around 3.45 p.m., thus ending Sepecat Jaguar operation in the UK.

On retirement XX833 had undertaken some 4,700 sorties, clocked up 5,335 flying hours with more than 7,690 landings. In the twelve years of service with MoD Boscombe Down, the aircraft had flown 1,070 hours, suffered five bird strikes, one lightning strike, consumed nine engines (with an average life of 122.33 hours each) and carried out over 864 sorties. Its final resting place was at RAF Cosford – the apparent retirement home for Jaguar aircraft.

No. 6 Squadron XZ392 seen in its Hardened Aircraft Shelter (HAS) at RAF Coningsby. Although the Jaguar utilised the HAS in Germany, the Coltishall squadrons operated from a normal flight-line, except when deployed to Bardufoss as part of their Air Forces North NATO commitment. The move to Coningsby brought with it hardened accommodation.

Above left: The abrupt end to RAF Jaguar operation saw a quick farewell held at RAF Coningsby in April 2007. Here XX112 in standard RAF tactical scheme stands as a backdrop with XX725 in a specially applied desert-pink scheme. XX725 had worn the Alkali Removable Temporary Finish (ARTF) version of this when deployed in the first Gulf War.

Above right: The squadron colours are paraded at the disbandment ceremony at RAF Coningsby with Jaguar GR.3A XX112 providing a fitting backdrop.

Right: The seven aircraft fly-past performs a break over the disbandment parade.

Wing Commander John Sullivan, OC No. 6 Squadron. The final RAF Jaguar squadron commander stands proudly against the 'Flying Canopeners' motif on XX725 at the disbandment ceremony on 31 May 2007.

Jaguar GR.3A XX725 – one of the most celebrated surviving Jaguar aircraft on the day of the squadron's disbandment, resplendent in a pseudo desert-pink scheme similar to that worn during 'Desert Storm'. Then the jet wore the code 'T' and the name *Johnny Fartpants* along with forty-seven mission symbols.

Right: A No. 6 Squadron Jaguar GR.3A (flown, it is believed, by Matt D'Aubyn) slices through the Cadair Idris pass in the Machynlleth Loop during the final month of Jaguar flying.

Below left: Jaguar GR.3A XX119 seen flying 'down in the weeds' on 2 February 2007 at a height that was typical in the aircraft's operating repertoire.

Below right: A Jaguar pulls hard out of the Bwlch pass, unusually sky-lining as it turns to head down through Cadair Idris on 9 October 2006.

Left: Even though the squadron had been 'down declared' the pilots had to maintain currency until such time as the aircraft could be delivered to RAF Cosford, their final resting place. As such, many 'general handling' sorties were flown during April and May 2007. Here a jet can be seen on the eastern edge of the Machynlleth Loop in LFA 7 taking the corner at Corris.

Below right: Seen in happier days is Jaguar GR.3A XZ392 'EM' of No. 6 Squadron high over the North Sea on 4 August 2005.

In this series of three shots the aircraft is seen entering the Machynlleth Loop from Bala. The shots highlight the aircraft's small radar signature and profile as it parallels the A487 road towards Tal-y-Llyn Lake.

On this page: Jaguar T.4 XX840 No. 6 Squadron low-level in Wales on 21 May 2007.

Opposite, top: The Jaguar's 'last hurrah' took place on 20 December 2007 when the QinetiQ two-seat XX833 undertook the type's final flight in RAF colours.

Opposite, bottom: XX833 pulls to begin the knife-edge through the Cader Idris pass.

ROYAL AIR FORCE OF OMAN (RAFO) JAGUARS

A FAREWELL FLY-PAST by four aircraft of the Royal Air Force of Oman (RAFO) on 6 August 2014 brought to a close another chapter in the history of the venerable Sepecat Jaguar aircraft. Presumably along with the type's retirement will be that of the RAF's last two Jaguar pilots, Wing Commander Craig Wilson and Squadron Leader Tony Hedley, both of whom were on 'loan service' to the RAFO.

In the case of Tony Hedley he had amassed more Jaguar flight hours than anyone else beating the previous incumbent, Dave Bagshaw, by quite a margin, having reached the magical 4,000 hours back in 2009.

These four aircraft were some of the very few still operational in the kingdom. In February 2014 the fleet reportedly comprised 200, 211, 213, 215, 219 and 222, which were serviceable, although 200 was apparently awaiting engines and 222 was down for a wing replacement, having flown a lot recently. Several others, thought to include 203, 209 and 210, were in store. So technically there were nine aircraft (A/C) still in service. However, in view of the short period of continued operation the unit had at that time effectively only six jets that were equipping solely No. 8 Squadron, No. 20 having stood down when the fleet was rationalised some time earlier.

Oman first received the Jaguar in March 1977. At the time, the air force was one of two anonymous export customers announced on 28 August 1974. The order was to comprise twelve Jaguar Internationals together with a pair of two-seat trainers, with deliveries commencing in March 1977 to equip a single squadron No. 8 at Masirah, identifiable by their red badge. Deliveries of these were undertaken by company pilots via Toulouse and Akrotiri.

A follow-on order was received for a further batch of aircraft in mid 1982 by which time two aircraft, one single seat and a dual, had been lost in accidents. As attrition replacement for the twin-seater aircraft XX138, at the time on loan to India, it was sold at the completion of its lease directly to Oman. The aircraft was, however, later flown to the UK for overhaul by the Jaguar Maintenance Unit (JMU) at Abingdon between September and December 1983.

The second batch of aircraft to equip No. 20 Squadron, identifiable by their blue badge, at the same base started being delivered in May 1983, with deliveries being completed by November of

Opposite: Jaguar OS 204 is seen over the desert in the Dhofar region of Oman.

Opposite: Nose-on profile of Jaguar OS 210 at Seeb during the annual month-long camp undertaken by all squadrons to the countries main airport.

that year. The two-twin seaters of this order, 213 and 214, were unique in both having the same ARI 18223 Radar Warning Receiver (RWR) as the single-seat versions and the only Warton-built aircraft to have French-type fixed in-flight refuelling probes.

The Need For A Close Air Support Ability Recognised

The Dhofar war, which was to last just over ten years, brought a sense of urgency into the creation of a well-equipped air force in Oman. In consequence twelve BAC 167 Strikemaster Mk 82 attack aircraft were ordered in May 1967 with deliveries commencing two years later.

Crewed mainly by RAF loan service pilots these versatile Counter-insurgency (COIN) aircraft were to shoulder the bulk of the air support for much of the Dhofar campaign, although losses began to mount as the Yemini forces began introducing more significant munitions into the fight. This led to an order of a further thirteen upgraded versions, but these arrived too late to influence the successful conclusion of the conflict.

Two main factors that were to bring the war to an end was Oman's ability to both resupply its forces by air (following the acquisition of three DHC-7 Caribou transport aircraft in 1970 along with the first six of an eventual sixteen Short Skyvan's and the first eight of an eventual fleet of forty Bell Iroquois helicopters) and the ability to give close air support.

Although the Strikemaster's performed admirably in this task King Hussein of Jordan made a gift of his entire remaining fleet of Hawker Hunter aircraft in February 1975. Again these thirty-one aircraft, a total eventually rising to thirty-eight, were at the outset crewed by RAF loan service personnel and were a significant factor in the turning point in the conflict. Equally, it is believed that other countries loaned a number of other assets during this period.

Above left: Prior to the building of the new base at Al Musanah to the north of Seeb, deploying units used the purpose-built shelters at the main airport. Here Jaguar OS 221 is seen at rest.

Above right: The RAFO Jaguars had a limited air-defence capability with air-to-air missiles (AAMs) on their over-wing rails. This was a daylight-only commitment, with the aircraft lacking radar. Here aircraft 202 is seen in the shelter at Seeb.

It was in the midst of the Dhofar Rebellion that Sultan Qaboos bin Said Al Said gained power following a coup in Oman. Although he was to be more progressive than his father he still had to deal with the legacy of the uprising of the Yemenie and Chinese-backed communist tribes in the Dhofar region.

Support came not only from the British but also Jordan and Iran before the People's Front for the Liberation of Oman (PFLO) was defeated in 1975.

The whole Dhofar campaign led to a rethink in strategy and structure of the Sultan's Armed Forces. In 1977 an Integrated Air Defence System was inaugurated with the arrival of the first twelve Sepecat Jaguar strike/attack aircraft, the introduction of two Rapier SAM (surface-to-air missile) squadrons and a comprehensive radar network. Shortcomings highlighted in the Dhofar campaign also led to the construction of Thumrait airfield so that both policing and support to the southern desert areas could be maintained.

Terrain in and around the capital at Seeb differs vastly from that surrounding the aircraft's operating base at Thumrait. Here 214 and 217 turn over the 'Jebel'.

New Base For Fast Jets

One of the principal upgrades to come out of the long-running conflict in Dhofar was the need for a base capable of operating all types of aircraft in defence of the region and, in particular, offer support to the oil industry. Arising out of this was Thumrait, a base not really very close to anywhere, and about a 90-minute drive from Salalah.

Built initially to operate Sultan of Oman Air Force's (SOAF's) fleet of Hawker Hunter fighters and later the Sepecat Jaguar, the base saw considerable upgrading at the time of the first Gulf War when US money introduced a number of improvements to permit Boeing B-52H operation. The United States had some 3,000 troops stationed in Oman during

Jaguar OB 214 leads Jaguar OS 217 on a sortie over the north of Oman during April 2006.

The mountain terrain
is ideal in providing
varied training and an
impressive backdrop.
The two-seater in this
shot, 214, had the
French-style refueling
probe, one of only two
produced like this at
the Warton factory.

that period. Thus, with a single main runway and two runway-width parallel taxi-ways, it is of a considerable size and was eventually to house RAFO's three main front-line squadrons.

No. 6 Squadron had formed in 1975 to operate the former Jordanian Hunters and was slated to become Oman's biggest single squadron with a unit establishment of thirty-eight aircraft, although a number of the jets received had been immediately cannibalised for spares. Losses over the near twenty-year period of operation amounted for over half the fleet with the remainder passing into retirement in 1994. Initially manned almost in its entirety by RAF loan service pilots SOAF gradually, with help, began altering the balance with home-produced aircrew. On 25 August 1988 aircraft 828 was lost in what was the first successful ejection by an Omani pilot.

The Hunter, apart from being considered one of the last pilot's aeroplanes, was a very exceptional ground-attack platform. In 1980 the aircraft was given added teeth when a number of the survivors

were upgraded to operate the AIM-9 Sidewinder AAM. In the end, however, the sheer age of the aircraft saw its retirement.

Eventually joining No. 6 Squadron at Thumrait was No. 8 Squadron equipped with the Sepecat Jaguar, which immediately gave RAFO a considerable increase in capability. Built to the Jaguar International specification the aircraft were fitted with over-wing missile rails and were tasked not only with ground attack but also air defence, a role it performed during daylight hours well into its career until the arrival of the air force's Lockheed Martin Block 50 F-16 Fighting Falcons.

A second squadron in the shape of No. 20 Squadron was formed in May 1983 equipped with aircraft built from the 1982 follow-on order, with deliveries of those jets being completed in November of that same year.

Attrition in the initial five years of operation was relatively high, necessitating the purchase of a number of second-hand aircraft as replacements. The first of these was the former RAF Jaguar T.2

Above left: Closest is Jaguar OS 217, flown by Squadron Leader Paul 'Skids' Harrison RAF, a loan service officer with RAFO during April 2006.

Above right: Led by Jaguar OB 214 with Jaguar OS 221 and 217, the formation is seen on a navigation exercise on a sortie from Seeb in April 2006. On 22 June 2010 221 was lost in an accident near Masirah.

Above: The same formation passing over one of the many restored forts in the north of the country.

Above right: Skirting around some of the peaks to the west of Seeb.

Opposite, top right: The coastline to the south of Seeb creates a magnificent backdrop to the two Jaguar aircraft. The deep blue azure of the sea is in great contrast to the browns of the mountains as they dip down towards the shore.

Opposite: 'Skids' Harrison makes a low approach in Jaguar OS 210 to the main taxiway at Thumrait in February 2009.

that had been on loan to India and this was passed directly onto Oman at the end of that period of loan in 1982. This was to be followed by two former RAF Jaguar GR.1s. The first was delivered in November 1986 and, more latterly, the second in August 1998. Both had been brought up to 'Jaguar 96' standard before delivery.

The whole fleet entered an upgrade to a similar standard and subsequently to 'Jaguar 97' configuration akin to the RAF Jaguar GR.3A, allowing it to deliver a far more wide-ranging selection of ordnance along with much improved navigation equipment.

Gone But Never Forgotten

Attrition continued to mount both through mishap and fatigue until, as aforementioned, at the beginning the force was down to a mere handful of aircraft. Its original out-of-service date (OSD) had been given as 2012 and it is due to the testament

of the maintenance personnel, both service and contract, that the fleet was kept on the front line for a further two years.

Although its passing is tinged with some sadness by all those associated with the type, its sell-by date was well overdue. With the arrival of a second squadron of F-16 Fighting Falcons at that time and the not too distant arrival of a squadron of Eurofighter Typhoons, the Oman Air Force is well equipped to play a pivotal role in the Middle East from its strategically important location for many years to come.

List of RAFO Jaguar Aircraft

200   T.2 ex XX138, JI 001. WFU (withdrawn from use) at Thumrait on November 2015.

201   OB G-27-278 F/F (first flight) 4 November 1976 (E. Bucklow/V. Malings) D/D (date delivered) 7 March 1977. W/O (written off) on 1 March 1981, 25 miles north of Thumrait. With No. 8 Squadron (flown by Bob Prest).

202 OS G-27-280 F/F 27 January 1977 (J. Lee) D/D 7 March 1977, G-BEET. WFU and stored at Thumrait in November 2010.

203 OB G-27-279 F/F 6 April 1977 (A. Love/J. Evans) D/D 27 June 1977, G-BETB. WFU and stored Thumrait August 2014.

204 OS G-27-281 F/F 18 May 1977 (E. Bucklow) D/D 27 June 1977. Involved in mid-air collision September 2013.

205 OS G-27-282 F/F 18 August 1977 (A. Love) D/D 26 September 1977. W/O 27 October 1991, 5 miles south of Masirah. With No. 20 Squadron.

206 OS G-27-283 F/F 19 August 1977 (T. Ferguson) D/D 26 September 1977. WFU at Thumrait by February 2009.

207 OS G-27-284 F/F 7 October 1977 (E. Bucklow) D/D 7 November 1977. W/O 17 December 1991, west of Jebel Abhdor Range following a bird strike. With No. 20 Squadron.

208 OS G-27-285 F/F 14 October 1977 (E. Bucklow) D/D 7 November 1977 W/O 31 December 1985.

With No. 20 Squadron (flown by Paddy Mullen).
209 OS G-27-286 F/F 16 December 1977 (E. Bucklow) D/D 6 February 1978. WFU by November 2010 at Thumrait.
210 OS G-27-287 F/F 12 January 1978 (P. Ginger) D/D 6 February 1978. WFU by November 2010 at Thumrait.
211 OS G-27-288 F/F 8 March 1978 (E. Bucklow) D/D 8 May 1978. WFU and GIA Seeb by August 2014.
212 OS G-27-289 F/F 31 March 1978 (E. Bucklow) D/D 8 May 1978. W/O 26 February 1979 after bomb exploded prematurely. With No. 8 Squadron (flown by Flight Lieutenant Rick Lea).
213 OB G-27-375 F/F 5 November 1982 (S. Aitken/K. Hartley) D/D 23 May 1983. WFU and GIA Seeb by August 2014.
214 OB G-27-376 F/F 26 November 1982 (P. Orme/L. Hurst) D/D 25 July 1983. W/O after landing short of the runway whilst night flying. Relegated to Damage Battle Repair (DBR) at Thumrait on 10 March 2014.
215 OS G-27-377 F/F 15 September 1982 (E. Bucklow) D/D 23 May 1983. WFU at Thumrait after collision with 223. GIA at Seeb by August 2014.
216 OS G-27-378 F/F 2 November 1982 (S. Aitken) D/D 23 May 1983. W/O 29 January 1991, 40 miles north-east of Thumrait.
217 OS G-27-379 F/F 7 January 1983 (S. Aitken) D/D 25 July 1983. W/O after mid-air collision September 2013. TT (total time) 3,532 hours. TL (total landings) 5,258.
218 OS G-27-380 F/F 12 May 1983 (C. Yeo) D/D 25 July 1983 W/O 21 June 1984 near Salalah with No. 8 Squadron (flown by Mohammed 'Mo').
219 OS G-27-381 F/F 26 April 1983 (E. Bucklow) D/D 19 September 1983. WFU and GIA MTC Seeb by August 2014.
220 OS G-27-382 F/F 18 May 1983 (C. Yeo) D/D 19 September 1983. W/O 11 September 2013 following a mid-air collision with 224.

221 OS G-27-383 F/F 1 June 1983 (P. Orme) D/D 19 September 1983. W/O 22 June 2010 near Masirah. TT 3315:30. TL 41619.
222 OS G-27-384 F/F 15 June 1983 (P. Gordon-Johnson) D/D 24 November 1983. Recieved new three-tone green/brown colour scheme. WFU Thrumthrait. TT 3,305 hours. TL 4,915.
223 OS G-27-385 F/F 7 July 1983 (E. Bucklow) D/D 24 November 1983. W/O following mid-air collision with 215? 3 November 2007. Stored Thumrait, February 2009.
224 OS G-27-386 F/F 15 July 1983 (E. Bucklow) D/D 24 November 1983. W/O 11 September 2013 following a mid-air collision with 220 with the loss of one pilot, Flight Lieutenant Al Azhar bin Hamad Al Shraiqi.
225 GR.1 ex XX740, JI 017 D/D 4 November 1986. WFU at Thumrait following a mid-air collision with, it is believed, 223.
226 GR.1 ex XX719 D/D 10 August 1998. W/O 1 May 2010.

Opposite: Jaguar OS 204 and 210 seen head-on whilst on a sortie from Thumrait in February 2009. The lead aircraft is clean whilst the trailing jet is fitted with two external wing tanks.

Above: Profile shot of Jaguar OS 217 inbound to Seeb in April 2006.

THE BEST IS STILL TO COME – INDIAN AIR FORCE JAGUARS

AS WE LAMENT the premature passing of the Jaguar in RAF service, and look around to see that in France, Ecuador, Oman and Nigeria the venerable lady has also been laid to rest, we could be forgiven in thinking that the sands of time were also running out with its last operator – India.

It may therefore come as a surprise to many that although Oman delayed its retirement until a suitable replacement was sourced, in India the type is not only still going from strength to strength but has only just recently finished production, the last aircraft coming off the line as late as early 2010. Should that, however, really be a surprise in a country where both the Royal Enfield motorcycle and the Austin Ambassador car were still in production!

India was the fifth nation to opt for the Jaguar to fulfil its interdictor deep-penetration strike role. That's not to say that it was late in considering the type, but that the whole bureaucratic system that engulfs India delayed its eventual procurement.

Akin with most negotiations that take place in India the sale was a protracted state of affairs and more than once nearly stalled. Beginning with first expressions of interest as early as 1966, followed by Wing Commander Prithi Singh having soloed in XW560 in June 1972, the deal was finally settled some twelve years later. In early 1975 an order for fifty aircraft was vetoed because India was requesting an unusually low rate. At the same time an approach by Libya for thirty-nine aircraft was also vetoed, whilst the interest by Turkey for twenty-four and Saudi Arabia for eighty to 100 came to nothing. In the following year Pakistan's interest in an initial order of six aircraft foundered on funding difficulties.

Finally Pen To Paper

Finally in September 1978 India selected Jaguar, or 'Shamsher' as it is known locally, to meet its deep-strike capability with an eventual requirement of 200 aircraft, although the Intent to Proceed (ITP) document was to cover only an initial 160. These were to be ordered in batches of twenty with the first forty to be built at Warton and the remainder under licence. On 21 October an ITP was signed by Sir Freddie Page for Sepecat and the Indian Defence Secretary, S.S. Banerji.

Opposite: The initial batch of Jaguar aircraft for India were built at the BAE facility at Warton and ferried to India. All were to the same standard as RAF aircraft of the day including the NAVWASS inertial navigation system and laser range finder fitted in the nose section, as is seen on JS110 here.

Above and opposite: The early aircraft all went to equip No. 5 Squadron (Tuskers) at Ambala, although they were eventually redistributed amongst other squadrons. Here JS110 is seen on its take-off run from Ambala.

attached to No. 54 Squadron at RAF Coltishall for 20 hours of tactical training before being declared limited combat-ready. A further eight pilots followed and these were to form the nucleus of IAF aircrew to oversee the type's induction into service.

First IAF Jaguar Unit Forms

No. 14 Squadron (Bulls) were the inaugural squadron to operate the Jaguar from Ambala Air Station. Previously a Hunter F.56A squadron, No. 14 was declared operational on the Jaguar in September 1980 shortly after the arrival of the last of the initial loan aircraft.

The forty Warton-produced aircraft were of a similar standard to the current RAF jets with Adour Mk 804E engines and NAVWASS avionics. The first delivery of these took place on 21 February 1981 with completion of the order in November 1982. These replaced the former RAF aircraft on loan to No. 14 Squadron but only after its co-located No. 5 Squadron (Tuskers) had been equipped.

The first aircraft of this batch, twin-seater JT051, was handed over on 10 February 1981 and delivered to India on 5 March. Deliveries of these forty BAE Systems-built aircraft were to continue until 6 November 1982 when the last aircraft JS135, in company with JS133, were delivered. No. 5 Squadron became operational on the type in the summer of 1981, and with the re-equipment of No. 14 Squadron running in parallel, it allowed for the return of the loan aircraft back to the UK.

This process commenced with the return of JI014 on 11 February 1982 and was completed on 19 April 1984 when the last five aircraft – JI007, 008, 010, 016 and 017 – were returned. JI007, the former XZ398 that had, incidentally, up until this point in time not entered service with the RAF, was used to integrate the Matra Magic AAM and in development trials of the Display Attack and Ranging Inertial Navigation (DARIN) system.

Given the leisurely pace of this decision the urgency to get the aircraft into squadron service was almost indecent. This resulted in the loan of eighteen RAF aircraft to equip No. 14 Squadron at Ambala. These loan aircraft consisted of sixteen Jaguar GR.1 (interim) and two Jaguar T.2 (interim) aircraft. The first two loan aircraft, one single seater and one twin, were handed over at Warton in a ceremony to the Indian Air Force (IAF) on 19 July 1979 and were flown to India a week later arriving in Ambala on 27 July. Flown by BAE Systems test pilots and Wing Commander Nadkarni IAF the jets were ferried via Toulouse, Brindisi, Luqa, Akrotiri, Seeb and Jamnager. The next two arrived on 14 October with the final deliveries occurring in August of the following year with all bar one aircraft being delivered by IAF pilots.

The first four IAF pilots commenced training at RAF Lossiemouth with No. 226 OCU on 26 February 1979 and, upon completion of the 45-hour course, were

Indigenous Production Begins

The first phase-three aircraft, JS136, built from Anglo-French Completely Knocked Down (CKD) kits by Hindustan Aeronautics Ltd (HAL) at Bangalore undertook its maiden flight on 31 March 1982, with the kit having been flown out to Bangalore on 5 May 1981. These differed from the earlier BAE-assembled examples, incorporating a more modern avionics suite known as DARIN. This featured a wide field-of-view Smiths General Electric Company) (GEC) Avionics Type 1301 HUDWAC (Head-Up Display & Weapon Aiming Computer), a GEC-Ferranti Combined Map & Electronic Display (COMED) 2045 , a SEGAM ULIS 82 INS and a Laser Ranger and Marked Target Seeker (LRMTS). All of this and other indigenous instrumentation were built around a MIL-STD-1553B digital databus, allowing for the integration of a wider range of stores, systems and ordnance. Power

also differed with the forty-five phase three aircraft – thirty-five single seat Jaguar IS and ten Jaguar IT – being fitted with the RT172-58 Adour Mk 811 engine, each rated at 8400lb of maximum thrust. The final CKD kit of the thirty-five Jaguar IS (JS136–JS170) and ten Jaguar IT (JT056–JT065) was received in Bangalore in March 1987.

The development of the DARIN inertial system began before delivery of even the first aircraft from BAE. The RAF had advised India that the Marconi NAVWASS equipment had very low reliability, to the extent that during operations no aircraft could be expected on the flight line after just a handful of sorties. The RAF were at this point intending to upgrade its aircraft with the Ferranti FIN 1024 INS and suggested that perhaps India would like to share development costs. However, as India was only being offered the FIN 1024E with inferior gyros to those proposed for the RAF aircraft this led India to

JS136 was one of the first HAL-built aircraft from knock-down kits supplied by BAE. It was this batch that was fitted with the DARIN inertial navigation and weapon-aiming system from inception. In this shot the slight re-profiling of the nose housing the laser range finder can be seen.

seek its own solutions. The IAF was forced to accept the standard NAVWASS in the direct supply aircraft, as there was no quick way in which to replace it.

Working with Sagem in France and in consultation with Aircraft & Systems Testing Establishment (ASTE) the major subsystems selected were Sagem inertial platform, Smiths Industries HUD/WUC, Ferranti COMED, Crouzet Air Data Package and SFIM Flight Test Instrumentation Package. All of these were integrated using the dual Mil 1553B standard digital databus with the Jaguar's Ferranti Laser Ranger and Marked Target Seeker retained.

To aid development two direct supply aircraft, JS102 and JS103, were loaned in 1981 for modification and trials. On completion of ground testing the first flight took place at Bangalore on 17 December 1982, from which is was concluded that the modified system was better than the 1 nautical mile per hour called for in the specification. Weapon-aiming accuracy and associated testing followed, resulting in an Initial Operating Clearance (IOC) in 1984 and Full Operating Clearance (FOC) a year later.

With the IOC being achieved in 1984 and FOC in 1985 the modification was gradually introduced in all

aircraft – these examples going to equip No. 16 (Cobras) Squadron in October 1986 and No. 27 (Flaming Arrows) Squadron in the summer of 1982, both at Gorakhpur and each with a unit establishment of sixteen strike and two twin-seat aircraft apiece.

The first all-Indian built Jaguar was scheduled from phase four with delivery in January 1988. Phase four had originally been planned as fifty-six aircraft of entirely local manufacture. Ultimately, however, according to BAE Systems this was to be later amended to a more modest total of thirty-one kits comprising twenty-three Jaguar IS (JS171–JS193) and eight Jaguar IM (JM251–JM258). This latter variant was unique in the Jaguar world, with a nose-mounted Agave radar that could be presented either in the HUD-up display or through the normal COMED display. Optimised for maritime air-to-surface operations, but with the ability to be utilised in the air-to-air mode, it could scan through 140 degrees azimuth and through 6 or 12 degrees in elevation (from a 60-degree arc).

The aircraft equipped one flight of No. 6 (Dragons) Squadron at Poona (now Pune). The variant first flew in 1985 and was handed over to the ASTE at Bangalore by HAL in January 1986. It, however, took a further seven years before all eight aircraft had been delivered at which time the IAF, under phase five, ordered a further batch of fifteen consisting of eleven Jaguar IS (JS194–JS205) and four Jaguar IM (JM259–JM262). The squadron also operated the IDS version of the Jaguar, drawn, it appears, also from the phase four production with the upgraded DARIN II avionics. However, the squadron was to relocate to Jamnagar in mid 2007 initially through runway repairs at the Pune base, but later as a permanent move, as the IAF restructured its front-line assets, although some sources state this was driven by airspace congestion in the area.

Interestingly in a report published by *TNN News* in India in February 2008 Wing Commander Satish Menon, PRO of South Western Air Command, which covers Pune and nearby areas, said that while one Jaguar squadron was already based in Jamnagar, one more was sanctioned some time back.

'The existing squadron in Jamnagar is for maritime defence and patrolling. The new squadron will be for

Above left: Although BAE is the design authority for the Jaguar, HAL at Bangalore have significant expertise in Jaguar building, upgrade and overhaul. The first seventy-nine single-seat aircraft and twelve two-seaters were all equipped with the standard DARIN system. Here JS180 is seen undergoing a major overhaul.

Above right: JT061 was one of twelve two-seaters built from scratch by HAL with the DARIN system. BAE had offered the Ferranti FIN 1024E INS to India but this was considered an inferior standard to that being fitted to the RAF jets. It was this that led to India considering an indigenous upgrade.

Four of five Jaguar aircraft opening the fly-past at Aero India led by two-seater JT063. The jets were operating from Bangalore but were from units assigned to Gorakhpur.

air defence over land,' said Menon. Does this suggest the much rumoured 'night interdiction squadron' has or was likely to be formed. In fact during 2008 No. 224 'Warlords' Squadron, the former MiG-23MF user, was believed to have reformed at Jamnagar on the Jaguar in just that role.

Again the aircraft in both phase four and phase five utilised the Adour 811 engine and incorporated the DARIN avionics suite. Deliveries were completed in 1999 and in March of the same year the IAF ordered an additional batch of seventeen Jaguar IT twin-seaters (JT066–JT082 (or JR11–JR27 in production)) for delivery commencing 2003. These were to be equipped with the upgraded DARIN II nav/attack system incorporating new Ring Laser Gyro/Inertial Navigation System (RLG/INS) with global positioning system (GPS), a new HUD and smart Multi-Functional Displays (MFDs) and employed jointly in operational training and the night-attack role utilising laser-guided weapons.

No. 6 Squadron (Dragons) are charged with Maritime Strike and as such are equipped to the Jaguar JM, which is fitted with the Thomson CSF Agave radar and the DARIN system. These twelve aircraft equip one flight of the squadron and others are equipped with standard interdiction aircraft. The jets were originally stationed at Pune but are now based at Jamnager. (Simon Watson)

Eight of the aircraft were delivered to the IAF by September 2004 and the remaining nine on 15 July 2005.

This batch of aircraft, however, caused some controversy when the IAF refused to fly two of the aircraft and declined to accept a further five due to the alleged use of non-standard parts. This, according to HAL, revolved around the use of the small BT nuts used in connecting the hydraulic systems. The larger nuts used are drilled for wire locking that is mandatory in the original specification. The smaller nuts were not drilled and therefore not wire locked. For some reason the batch of small BT nuts used in the construction of these Jaguar ITs had erroneously been drilled but, in accordance with the laid-down procedure, were not wire locked. It was the discovery of these BT nuts with holes that caused concerns and the seven aircraft involved had to be returned to HAL for a complete replacement with the approved materials.

Final Production In Sight

The final order for Jaguar came on 31 March 2006 when phase six's twenty single-seat Jaguar IS were funded and would keep the aircraft in production initially until 2008, although in fact it was to be until 2010. This final batch of aircraft (JS206–JS225) were to be also equipped with the upgraded DARIN II nav/attack system, a new LRMTS and the incorporation of the ELTA-built airborne, self-protection jammer and an indigenous radar-warning receiver within the aircraft's electronic countermeasure (ECM) suite. However, there has been some confusion over the actual amount of units delivered. The Jaguar IS aircraft, and this includes the maritime versions, have build numbers running from JQ001 to JS136 and run consecutively with a few exceptions, caused presumably by delays in individual CKD kit arrivals. Although, HAL, by their own omission, state that the

final aircraft from phase four is JQ081 or JS205 in IAF service. However, seventy IDS and twelve maritime equate to eighty-two aircraft suggesting that one example or serial does not exist. This was supported with the confirmation that JS209 from phase five is in fact JQ085. Equally BAE Systems records show JQ08 and JQ09 being out of sequence as JS153 and JS146 respectively whilst JS139, the fourth aircraft of the CKD batch, as JQ05, indicating that there was an additional airframe built and not used.

It was thought that this additional batch would allow for the equipping of a sixth front-line Jaguar squadron to be used, possibly in a night attack, in a specialised target marking and designation role. As aforementioned No. 224 Squadron was reported to have reformed at Jamnagar with this role in mind, although new build aircraft have been going to current squadrons and the first five aircraft from

phase six had been delivered to No. 14 Squadron by February 2007. Deliveries by October 2007 had reached JS212 with JS213 awaiting acceptance, leaving twelve aircraft still to be delivered. Production was expected to cease in late 2008 but ultimately extended through to early 2010 with the last four aircraft, JQ098–JQ101 (JS222–JS225), bringing an end to Jaguar production that had started thirty-six years previously.

Above: JS136 seen at Hindon during the Indian Air Force's 75th anniversary celebrations.

Opposite: JT066.

Above: Two-seater JT066 was the first IAF aircraft to be fitted with the DARIN II upgraded inertial system and is seen here at Aero India in Yelahanka.

Opposite: This cockpit shot of JS108 shows the original NAVWASS concept of the direct-sale aircraft. All of the survivors of this batch have now been upgraded with the DARIN II system.

Mid-Life Upgrade To Single Common Standard

Upgrade of the remaining Jaguar fleet was seen as a priority and contracts were signed with Sextant of France and Elta of Israel to upgrade the avionics of the 'strike' Jaguars. In 2009 the twenty-seven survivors of the thirty-five BAE-built NAVWASS-equipped aircraft were reported to have all been upgraded with the Darin II avionics package and it was expected, but is not clear whether funded, that the DARIN I HAL-built aircraft would be the first batch of aircraft to enter the future upgrade programme, although JS136

displayed at the IAF 70th anniversary had clearly received the DARIN II upgrade.

The DARIN III and avionics upgrade of these aircraft is expected to see the Sextant fourth-generation ring-laser-gyro-based inertial navigation system with embedded global positioning system at the core giving a very high mean time between failures (MTBF) with constant accuracy; a new head-up display (HUD) with upfront control panel with a greater field of view; a Sextant MFD 66 active matrix liquid crystal smart multifunction display (SMFD) for day/night readability with AMLCD 6 × 6 display with map and chart overlay, along with electronic warfare (EW) data;

a mission computer dual in hot standby mode to give high computing accuracy, high-speed processing incorporating a large memory for growth; an air-data package, digital map generator, data transfer system, upgraded radio altimeter, colour charge-coupled device (CCD) video camera with 90 minutes of recording time over a multi-channel digital recording system; new laser ranging marked target seeker, indigenous RWR integrated with ECM and internal self-protection jammer. Interestingly, the first aircraft to receive the DARIN III upgrade was that of a maritime version, although these did not feature in the DARIN II programme. The first jet modified was JM255 and it undertook its first flight in this configuration on 28 November 2012, although the IAF was reportedly unhappy with the improvements.

The IAF had assigned three airframes to the DARIN III upgrade programme: JM255, as described above, along with a JS and JT interdiction strike examples. HAL had gone back to the drawing board following the concerns shown by the IAF and on 25 March 2015, according to their spokesman Gopel Suttar, reported that the company had successfully flight-tested two of the Jaguar aircraft equipped with the advanced DARIN III systems. The first flight had lasted 15 minutes and the second for 1 hour. An initial batch of sixty Jaguars are planned to undergo DARIN III upgrade as soon as the test and evaluation is completed.

There are also plans for a new laser designator pod to enhance the night-attack capability and it is widely expected that this would be the Litening laser designation pod, which would infer the need for a new stick-top and hand controller to give a greater hands-on throttle and stick (HOTAS) functionality.

In September 2008 the general manager of HAL's Aircraft Design and Research Centre, P.L. Vaishampayan, reported that the company had successfully completed the first phase of the upgrade programme for the Jaguar aircraft and delivered the fleet to IAF (as described earlier).

JAGUAR COCKPIT LAYOUT'S

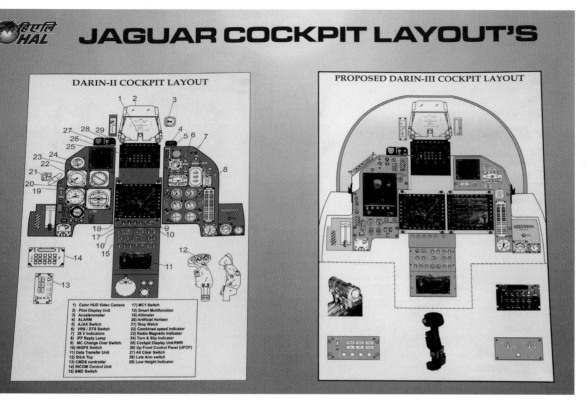

DARIN-II COCKPIT LAYOUT

PROPOSED DARIN-III COCKPIT LAYOUT

1) Color HUD Video Camera	17) MC1 Switch
2) Pilot Display Unit	18) Smart Multifunction
3) Accelerometer	19) Altimeter
4) ALARM	20) Artificial Horizon
5) AJAX Switch	21) Stop Watch
6) VRS / DTS Switch	22) Combined speed indicator
7) 26 V Indicators	23) Radio Magnetic Indicator
8) IFF Reply Lamp	24) Turn & Slip Indicator
9) MC Change Over Switch	25) Cockpit Display Unit RWR
10) INGPS Switch	26) Up Front Control Panel (UFCP)
11) Data Transfer Unit	27) All Clear Switch
12) Stick Top	28) Late Arm switch
13) CMDS controller	29) Low Height Indicator
14) INCOM Control Unit	
15) SMD Switch	

Above left: This HAL-produced schematic shows the current DARIN II concept being retrofitted into all IAF Jaguar aircraft when on major overhaul and the proposed DARIN III future upgrade. To date no formal decision has been taken on this upgrade that may be combined with the installation of a new engine as well. However, the IAF has loaned three aircraft to HAL for initial installation and testing.

Vaishampayan said the upgrade programme included a new version of avionics as well other features, which would make the planes more lethal for the long-range ground-attack operation ('the upgrade programme has added more teeth to the fleet's striking capability'). The main focus of the future upgrade programme was to replace the older version of the avionics in the aircraft with a new version, known as display attack ranging inertial navigation (DARIN III).

The HAL is also believed to be carrying out another development programme for the Jaguar fleet that includes additional features like an advanced radar system.

'Another development programme is going on for the strike aircraft to add some additional features like advanced radar systems which IAF wants,'

Vaishampayan said. The additional development programme for the fleet is being carried out by the Bangalore-based defence behemoth in consultation with the IAF.

A variety of weapons including cluster, free fall and laser-guided bombs, as well as rockets, can be carried on the four wing stations of the aircraft, which is also capable of carrying nuclear warheads.

It was also the intention to upgrade the maritime Jaguar IMs and a contract was reported to have been signed with Elta in 1996 to upgrade the aircraft with the EL/M-2032 multi-mode fire control radar. This may not have occurred, with the need to upgrade the main force seen as a priority. Certainly at HAL Bangalore in October 2007 there was no evidence of this work as being ongoing, although there were six NAVWASS Jaguar IS aircraft in for the DARIN II and

Avionics upgrade. In September 2006 it was announced that the IAF had issued a request for proposal (RFP) for a long-range anti-ship missile to replace its aging Sea Eagle. Likely bidders were thought to be Boeing with Harpoon and MBDA with Exocet. That said, HAL stated in February 2009 that they had completed the series compliance of ELTA FCR modification on the surviving ten Jaguar Maritime aircraft.

HAL has also recently completed the retrofit of a twin-seat Jaguar, JT068, from the final HAL-built batch with DARIN II avionics with an in-flight refuelling probe. The probe is a fixed mount unlike that of the single-seat aircraft. It also differs from the probe fitted to the Adla and Omani Jaguars and is more in keeping with that of the Dassault Mirage 2000. Whether this modification will be rolled out fleet-wide or just confined to a limited number of jets, presumably for the 'possible' new No. 224 Squadron, is not clear.

New Engine Required

These modifications are thought to only be a first phase in the long-term future of the venerable Jaguar in IAF service. Certainly there are further thoughts and perhaps the upgrade of the maritime aircraft will occur in phase two. However, with the need to extend the life of the Jaguar for possibly fifteen to twenty years the engine is another major factor in the continuing saga of Jaguar. All operators have complained about the lack of power as supplied by the Adour, especially in hot and high conditions, and this is particularly noticeable in the Mk 804E-engined example. My own experiences in Oman became clear

Above left: JS177 undergoing a major overhaul with HAL at their Bangalore facility.

Above right: The final batch of twenty 'strike' aircraft built by HAL at their Bangalore facility had DARIN II fitted as standard. Here JQ099, a HAL-build sequence number, is seen on final assembly back in 2010. The jet was to become JS223 in IAF service.

No. 5 Squadron (Tuskers) aircraft, JS134, seen at its Ambala base. The jet was one of the direct supply aircraft from BAE but, as can be seen from the nose profile, has received the DARIN II upgrade. This jet was the penultimate aircraft to be supplied by the Warton/Samlesbury facility.

in my mind as I accelerated along Seeb International Airport's main runway with the end getting awfully close before we reached V1.

In India the IAF was considering in early 2007 the possibility of re-engining the jet – the figure quoted as 126 aircraft – with the Honeywell F125IN power plant. This engine offers a 9 per cent increase in dry thrust over the Adour Mk 811 and a 12 per cent increase in burner. However, thoughts appeared at one time to have turned towards the Adour Mk 821 that takes the cold section of the Mk 811 and the hot section of the Mk 951 of the Hawk Mk 132 to give an additional 15 per cent of thrust.

No decision was believed to have been taken, but as the aircraft gets heavier an engine upgrade would have to be considered at some point. The DARIN III upgrade is set to cause additional weight problems, as the Jaguar IS/IT variants, unlike the Jaguar IM, do not currently possess a built-in radar system. The weight and thrust issues are further exacerbated not only by India's 'hot and high' conditions but also by the fact that the IAF now employs the Jaguar in the medium-level role, one it was never designed to fulfil, and quite simply the aircraft runs out of thrust in some profiles.

IAF had actually issued an RFP, or tender, in November 2010 to Rolls-Royce, which had provided the Adour 102 engines when the aircraft were acquired at the beginning of 1978 from the then British Aircraft Corporation (BAC) and the US Honeywell, which says it has offered to supply 'more powerful engines at competitive rates'.

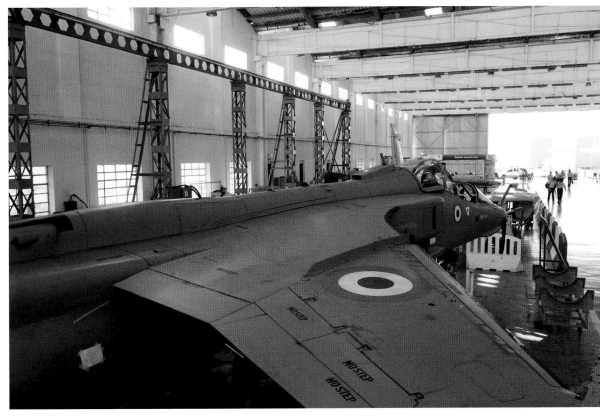

A further upgrade being undertaken by HAL is the fitment of an in-flight refueling probe to the two-seat aircraft. In 2009 JT068, one of the final batch of two-seaters produced, had been retrofitted with a fixed probe and is seen here at the HAL Bangalore facility.

In 2009 Rolls-Royce had successfully tested its upgraded Adour Mk 821 on an RAF Jaguar GR.3A at RAF Cosford in the presence of an IAF delegation. However, in March 2011 they opted out of the bidding process when the IAF issued an RFP for a more powerful power pack, leaving the IAF with a single vendor situation; in consequence the MOD cancelled the RFP.

Air Chief Marshal Naik at the time said the government was now considering processing the case on the 'single vendor' basis, keeping in view what was available, and most suited, and negotiate with the selected manufacturer. Nonetheless, after dithering over this proposal for two years a fresh engine tender was issued in October 2012 and once again only Honeywell were the sole bidder.

The Indian MoD, however, still appeared undecided in spite of the fact that the government had stated in parliament that the Jaguar upgrade would be completed by December 2017!

Honeywell for their part had acquired a surplus RAF Jaguar – former XX737 and ironically interim IAF loan aircraft JI015 – from Everett Aerospace in the UK. In this jet they had retrofitted it with the F125IN engine and had successfully flown them – thus giving them the confidence to pursue the IAF contract.

In the meantime attrition in the Jaguar world simply by the nature of its operating environment was likely to be high, although the twin-engine concept gave a good measure of survivability. Alas, when things go wrong at low-level this will often lead to the loss of an aircraft.

However, in the spring of 2016 the IAF confirmed that it will re-engine its fleet of Anglo-French Jaguar strike aircraft. The plan was discussed by IAF Chief of Air Staff Arup Raha during his annual press conference. He confirmed Honeywell is to supply 270 F125IN turbofan engines to replace the twin Rolls-Royce Adour Mk 815 on approximately 120 Jaguars. The F125 is 600lb lighter and should enable 25 per cent shorter hot and high take-offs. Raha said: 'India's Jaguars have become overweight and underpowered because of avionics and systems upgrades. Honeywell will first be required to conduct a trial modification of the Jaguars with the new engines.'

Attrition At Acceptable Levels

The RAF were to lose sixty-seven aircraft (29 per cent of the overall fleet) in thirty-four years of operational service – a loss of less than 1 per cent per year which, given its role, is not overly high. France, which was to receive slightly less aircraft, was to lose sixty-two (31 per cent) over thirty-two years, which is comparable. In India the air force has operated the Jaguar since 1979 (thirty-seven years) and attrition is estimated at forty (see list below); in other words, just over one a year or 20 per cent of the fleet out of 167 aircraft that operated – this figure also includes the interim loan aircraft. This signifies a very good safety record in a country that sees lots of large birds at low-level, which are never a fighter pilot's best friend especially when viewed against MiG-21 losses.

Chronology Of IAF Losses

16 April 1981 JI006 – Crashed following a bird strike. Flight Lieutenant Adhikari ejected safely.

10 April 1982 JI011 – Crashed when it flew into a hill. No. 14 Squadron pilot Flight Lieutenant R.K. Shrivastava was killed.

19 October 1983 JS125 – Crashed at Hissar. Flown at the time by Flight Lieutenant A.K. Bugnait.

11 April 1984 JS114 – Crashed. Flown at the time by Flight Lieutenant G.S. Atwal.

1 June 1984 JS104 – Crashed. Flown at the time by Squadron Leader G. Singh.

7 August 1984 JS122 – Crashed. Flown at the time by Flight Lieutenant P.V. Deshpandi.

27 February 1985 JS... – Crashed (also reported as 1 March 1985). Flown at the time by Squadron Leader G. Singh.

17 October 1985 JS... – Crashed. Flown by Flight Lieutenant J.S. Walia.

27 May 1986 JS... – Crashed. Flown at the time by Flight Lieutenant A.C. Bharali.

30 August 1987 JS... – Crashed at Kounour on take-off from Blore. Aircraft with ASTE and flown by Wing Commander Ashok Yadav at the time.

10 December 1987 JS... – Crashed on a night low-level sortie. No. 6 Squadron aircraft flown by Flight Lieutenant S.D. Bajpal.

3 March 1989 JS150 – Crashed on landing following what was thought to be a bird strike. No. 14 Squadron aircraft burnt out on the ground.

6 June 1989 JS... – Crashed at Barur (Tamil Nadu) with the loss of the ASTE pilot, Squadron Leader Karve.

1 August 1990 JS... – Crashed near Deoria, Utter Prudesh following mid-air collision. No. 16 Squadron.

Opposite: Engine upgrade is high on the agenda for improving the Jaguar further. However, although a sound proposal the Honeywell F125 engine is the only bidder for the contract and India seems unhappy with going with the single bidder concept.

Above: Honeywell purchased surplus ex-RAF Jaguar GR.3A XX737 from Everett Aerospace back in 2008 and retrofitted the aircraft with a pair of F125 engines to prove the concept. The jet has been successfully flown and tested from their Phoenix facility.

Opposite: Direct sale but upgraded Jaguar JS134 of No. 5 Squadron (Tuskers) seen outside a shelter at its Ambala base in October 2007.

1 August 1990 JS... – Crashed near Deoria, Utter Prudesh, following mid-air collision. Both aircraft from No. 16 Squadron.

25 August 1991 JS... – Crashed at Gorakhpur. Flying Officer Rana killed.

22 October 1993 JS120 – Crashed at Naraingar following a double hydraulic failure. Flight Lieutenant P.K. Pareek ejected safely.

1 June 1994 JT0... – Crashed at Gorakhpur following control restriction. Aircraft possibly salvageable utilising parts from another crash from 1994. Aircraft from No. 16 Squadron.

22 March 1995... – Crashed on take-off from Ambala.

25 June 1995 JS161 – Crashed on landing at Gorakhpur after tail chute deployed. Flight Lieutenant Chauhan ejected safely.

16 October 1995 JS... – Crashed at low level on flight from Ambala. Flying Officer R. Singh killed.

17 October 1995... – Crashed close the India/Pakistan border at Rajasthan.

22 November 1995 JS120 – Crashed.

16 February 1996 JS167 – Crashed on a flight test after

Above: HAL-built JS136 seen at Hindan for the 75th anniversary of the IAF displaying a full selection of weapons available.

Opposite: Direct supply Jaguar JS102 seen at Bangalore on DARIN II upgrade in 2007. This aircraft, along with JS103, were utilised in the original DARIN upgrade programme in 1981. The first flight with the new system took place on 17 December 1982 at the ASTE facility at Bangalore.

engine modification near Kurmi Village, Gorakhpur. Flight Lieutenant Navneet Raina of No. 16 Squadron ejected safely.

13 August 1996 JS167 – Crashed on take-off from Ambala. See previous crash.

26 February 1997 JT066 – Crashed near Uttarlai following a total electrical failure and engine flame out. Flight Lieutenant P.K. Pareek ejected safely.

16 February 1999 JM2... – Crashed at Pune when it failed to get airborne. Flight Lieutenant Agarwal survived the incident and aircraft probably repairable.

30 June 1999 JS... – Crashed in Punjab region near villages of Changera and Killaurin Patiala district. Flight Lieutenant Modak of No. 14 Squadron ejected safely.

20 September 1999 JS... – Crashed into buildings in Gorakhpur, Uttar Prudesh. The pilot from No. 16 Squadron ejected safely.

7 November 1999 JS... – Crashed on sortie from Gorakhpur near Sidhwapar. The pilot from No. 16 Squadron ejected safely.

25 October 2001 JS... – Crashed near Meerut. Flight Lieutenant Romesh Sharma of No. 5 Squadron ejected safely.

9 May 2002 JS139 – Crashed on take-off from Ambala with the loss of the pilot, Flying Officer S. Paliwal (date also quoted as 2003).

5 November 2002 JS... – Crashed at Dalipgarh near Ambala, killing a reported six people on the ground. Pilot, Flight Lieutenant Rehani from No. 14 Squadron, ejected but suffered spinal injuries.

28 January 2003 JS... – Crashed over Mahrajan firing range in Bikaner district with the loss of the No. 5 Squadron pilot, Wing Commander Mukhopadhyay.

22 July 2003 JS... – Crashed on take-off at Ambala following an in-flight fire. The pilot, Flight Lieutenant S. Kanvinde from No. 5 Squadron, died in the crash despite being rescued by crash rescue team.

26 February 2004 JS... – Crashed near Chandhan range at Pokhran with loss of No. 6 Squadron pilot, Wing Commander Ravi Khanna.

2 April 2004 JS... – Crashed in Himalayas, northern Kashmir following a mid-air collision with another Jaguar with loss of pilot, Flight Lieutenant Gagan Oberoi from Ambala.

2 April 2004 JS... – Crashed in Himalayas, northern Kashmir with loss of pilot, Flight Lieutenant Mayank Mayur of No. 5 Squadron from Ambala.

7 May 2004 JS148 – Crashed near Ambala at Patti Shekhanwith, the No. 5 Squadron pilot, Squadron Leader Tamasker, ejecting safely.

Fly-past of five No. 14
Squadron IAF Jaguars
at Aero India in 2010.

11 May 2005 JS202 – Crashed 18.64 miles north-west of Gorakhpur shortly after take-off. The No. 16 Squadron pilot, Flight Lieutenant Amit Singh, was killed. (Also reported as JS204.)

5 October 2005 ... – Crashed. Aircraft from Gwalior.

7 October 2005 JS... – Crashed on outskirts of Gwalior, the pilot Squadron Leader V. Gupta ejected safely.

18 January 2007 JS... – Crashed at the Pokhran firing range in Rajasthan with the loss of pilot, Flight Lieutenant Sirao, whilst operating from Nal Air Station.

26 October 2007 ... – Crashed on take-off from Jamnagar. Pilot, Squadron Leader Sangwan, ejected safely. Presumably a No. 6 Squadron aircraft.

4 August 2011 JS197 – Crashed near Dilahi Firozpur Villade, Mau District. Flown by Flight Lieutenant Saiihartha A. Pandey, No. 16 Squadron.

6 November 2012 JT061 – Crashed. Cat 3 (considered beyond economical repair).

30 November 2012 JS... – Crashed into a forest near Lik in Upper Dzongu in North Sikkim. Flown by Flight Lieutenant Yogesh Yadav No. 27 Squadron.

22 January 2014 JT067 – Crashed.

5 March 2015 JS... – Crashed in Kurukshetra District on a flight from Ambala. Flight Lieutenant Vivek Chaudhary ejected.

16 June 2015 JT060 – Crashed 11.18 miles from Allahabad. Pilot ejected.

Left: One of the
four No. 14 (Bulls)
Squadron aircraft
undertaking a tactical
demonstration at the
IAF's 75th anniversary
celebration held
at Hindan air base
close to Delhi in
October 2007.

Below left: During April
2016 the IAF undertook
its second Red Flag
deployment, this
time in Alaska. It took
with it four Sukhoi
Su-30MKI aircraft and
four Sepecat Jaguars –
JS209, 210, 221 and
222. A pair are seen
here on this official
IAF photo with their
attendant IL.78 tanker
en route from India.

N.B. Attrition details courtesy of *British Aviation Review*, Mach III publications and Warbirds of India.

It is expected that the Jaguar will remain in service for at least another decade, and whilst we mourn the passing of this venerable aircraft in the UK it still has copious amounts of Eastern promise! Its future will, however, possibly be determined by the recent announcement of an order for the Dassault Rafale. Reports indicate that the airbase at Ambala will be one of the first recipients of this down-market Typhoon.

In the meantime Jaguar forms an important part of the IAF's strike package. To demonstrate this the air force deployed nine Jaguars to Red Flag in the United States for a two-month period in early 2006 and, more recently, a mixed force of Jaguar and Sukhoi Su-30MKI fighters to Red Flag Alaska in April 2016. A major logistical event but one that

proves even after several decades of service the Jaguar is still at the forefront of IAF thinking. Six aircraft also undertook Exercise Eastern Bridge in Thumrait, Oman in October 2009.

FAE JAGUARS

Ecuador, The Sepecat Jaguar And 'Tarnish 9' Reunited With FAE Jaguar 327

The Fuerza Aérea Ecuatoriana withdrew its Sepecat Jaguar aircraft from its front-line inventory in September 2002 and placed the surviving aircraft into warm storage at its Taura base, pending a final decision as to whether to withdraw the type altogether or return them to service following a significant upgrade and overhaul. Twelve years down the road the airframes had deteriorated to such a degree in the hot and humid atmosphere of the Amazonian climate that any decision to return these to service had effectively been taken out of the hands of any decision makers.

On 11 October 2014 former BAE Production Test Pilot Eric Bucklow was reunited with Sepecat Jaguar No. 327 of the Ecuadorean Air Force, a jet that he delivered to the country over thirty-seven years previously.

Four of the twelve aircraft delivered were lost in accidents and of the remainder two are in 'preservation' whilst the others are languishing on their former home airfield at Taura.

As for 327, this departed the BAE facility at Warton on 16 August 1977 in the hands of John Cockburn, another Warton Test Pilot. The delivery flight to Taura was to involve some 16 hours 35 minutes total flight time spread over ten days. John Cockburn flew the first leg from Warton to Toulouse lasting 1 hour 30 minutes whilst Eric Bucklow, 'Tarnish 9', flew aircraft 329. These were the first two aircraft to be ferried to Ecuador by company pilots, with the earlier deliveries having been undertaken by Fuerza Aérea Ecuatoriana (FAE) pilots.

After a night stop the pair of Jaguars departed Toulouse for Dakar by way of Agadir with a flight time of 4 hours 30 minutes. Eric was by this time flying 327, the reason for the change of mounts lost in the depths of time. The following day the pair left Dakar for Ascension, refueling en route in Monrovia.

After a good rest (well after attending the garrison commander's party) the aircraft set out from Ascension on their single-longest leg across the Atlantic to Recife on the Brazilian coast. Lasting some 2 hours 25 minutes with nowhere in which to divert this was at the extremity of the Jaguar's range and no doubt perhaps the most worrying leg of the delivery flight.

Opposite: Aircraft 302 displayed on the approach road to the Air Force Academy at Salinas.

Above left: Ecuador had taken its Jaguar aircraft out of service prior to their demise with the RAF. The jets were, however, kept in warm storage at Taura for a number of years until finally pensioned off. Several were then moved to museums including 327 (above right) with the national collection in Quito.

Opposite, top right: The Jaguar was well liked and respected by its pilots and its capabilities were also well respected by its neighbours.

Opposite, bottom: Former BAE test pilot Eric Bucklow is seen here reunited with 327, an aircraft that he delivered from the UK with its epic oversea flight.

The two pilots took a well-earned three-day break in Recife before setting off northwards to Belem and then on to Trinidad, the two legs equalling some 4 hours 15 minutes in the air. From Trinidad it was on to Maracay in Venezuela, which was just a 1-hour short hop before the final leg of 2 hours 15 minutes on 25 August down to Taura.

Eric Bucklow's association with aircraft 327 was not just that delivery flight, as he had also been the pilot of the jet's first flight on 1 April 1977, then of course operating as UK 'B' registration G-27-272.

Escuadron de Combat (Esc) 2111 of Ala 21 at Taura were to only operate the Jaguar for a relatively short period of time (in comparison with other operators), although at perhaps one of the most important periods in the country's recent history when the jet gave the air force an important deep-penetration attack capability in its border struggles with Peru during the 1981 'Protocolo War'. The FAE was careful and its fighters seldom ventured anywhere near the combat zone. This was proven in late January 1981 when a Mirage F.1 flown by Lieutenant Colonel William Birkett Mórtola came under the attack of Peruvian SAMs

and had to evade by a hard manoeuvre. Ecuadorian Jaguars were held back: their sole contribution to the fighting was a mission aimed to find a Peruvian radar station set up in the north-western Amazon region. Flown by Captain César Naranjo Anda at a very low level and deep into the Peruvian airspace, the results of this sortie were considered as successful, but subsequently the Jaguars were put in reserve and – although their crews were briefed for possible attacks against FAP airfields – did not fly any combat sorties. It is believed, however, that the aircraft were retained as a strategic threat in case the conflict escalated but they never undertook any such missions.

The decision to buy the Sepecat Jaguar came following a visit by the Ecuadorean commander-in-chief in September 1972 and the detail of the sale only came to light on 28 August 1974 when BAC announced that it had secured export orders for undisclosed customers. Confirmation that these export orders were from Ecuador and Oman surfaced not long after. The contract from Ecuador was reportedly for $65 million inclusive of spares, support and initial training.

Shortly after, the FAE in co-operation with the RAF sent six pilots to RAF Lossiemouth to begin conversion to the type with No. 226 Operational Conversion Unit (OCU). This ten-month course began in January 1977 and on completion saw the newly qualified pilots undertake delivery of the final two aircraft.

Throughout the type's operational service in Ecuador pilots regularly returned to the OCU to undertake periodic check rides and emergency procedure updates utilising the units simulator facility, as Ecuador had opted for this seemingly less expensive option rather than the expense of procuring a simulator of their own. Oman undertook a similar package of training.

The aircraft acquired by Ecuador were to a similar standard to the RAF version, with fin-mounted ARI 18223 RWR and nose LRMTS, whilst adopting a similar camouflage pattern that fitted in well with the Amazonian jungle terrain that it would be operating over. The armament carried was similar to what was employed by the RAF at the time although the FAE aircraft were cleared to operate the MATRA

550 Magic AAMs from the over wing rails. Principal weapons included the internal pair of DEFA 30mm cannon with a fire rate of 150 rounds per minute, the general-purpose Mark 82 bomb, BL755 cluster bombs and MATRA rocket pods, all of which were carried on the five external stations up to a maximum payload of 4,500kg.

The jets were, however, powered at the outset by the uprated RT172-26 Adour engine, or Mark 804 as they were usually known, that were nominally rated at 5,620lb st (25 kN) dry and 8,000lb st (36 kN) in reheat. The engine eventually also began replacing the older less powerful Mk 102s in RAF jets. This engine provided a 27 per cent thrust increase at sea level at speeds between Mach 0.8 and 0.9 – a 10 per cent improved take-off and 30 per cent sustained turn capability over the earlier Mk 102.

The first Ecuadorean aircraft, the two-seat FAE283, undertook its maiden flight on 19 August 1976 in the hands of T. Ferguson and J. Evans. Eric Bucklow was to undertake the maiden flights of six of the FAE aircraft: 302, 305, 327, 329, 340 and 348. The deliveries commenced on 4 January 1977 with jets

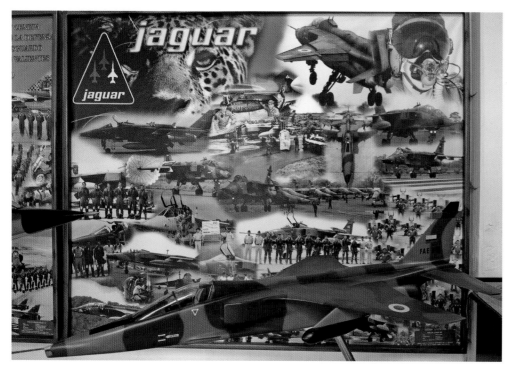

Above left: A mural within the Quito Museum dedicated to the FAE Jaguar force.

Above right: A mural on the wall at Cotopaxi, the FAE's main aircraft overhaul facility.

283 and 289. These continued in pairs during April, May, August and September with the last two departing Warton on 24 October 1977.

As said earlier four jets were lost in accidents all relatively early in the type's career in Ecuador. Following the fourth incident on 29 March 1990, which saw the loss of aircraft 289 some 34km from Guayaquil, BAC (now BAE Systems) either proposed or were asked to look at supplying replacement aircraft from the RAF's surplus stock. In consequence RAF jets XX121 and XX722 were withdrawn from store at RAF Shawbury and shipped to the Warton facility. A third aircraft, XX744, was also inspected for overhaul as well, whilst the option on three further aircraft was considered. However, by July 1993 the deal had failed to materialise and the aircraft were returned to store.

By 2000 Esc 2111, the squadron component of Gruppo 211, was only operating six aircraft: single-seat 302, 309, 327 and 329 along with both twin-seaters 283 and 305. Single-seat 339 and 348 were in storage. Although well liked by the pilots and well respected by its neighbours the writing was by this time already on the wall, with the dual-rolled Kfir C2 aircraft having been upgraded to 'CE' standard giving it a greater operational effect. The Mirage F.1JAs were also adequately providing the country's air-defence cover, with the threat from the south having effectively receded. It particularly receded following the aerial victories by Mirage F.1JA 807 flown by Major Raul Banderas and Captain Carlos Uzcategui Soli flying 806 over a pair of Peruvian Sukhoi Su-20M 'Fitter 'F'' on 10 February 1995 during the 'Condor War'. The trio of types had been well equipped, with well-trained crews having enjoyed an enviable reputation throughout South America for more than two decades.

The Jaguar was therefore withdrawn from front-line service in 2002 and the remaining aircraft placed in

'warm storage' where they remained for the next four years until officially declared withdrawn in 2006.

Today 302 is on display at the air force academy at Salinas whilst 327 is part of the national collection in Quito. The other jets still survive, four of which – 283, 309, 329 and 348 – serve as decoys at Taura, whilst 305 and 339 are maintained sheltered in a respectable status pending an uncertain future.

For Eric Bucklow being reunited with an aircraft that was probably his most significant Jaguar flight across the Atlantic was an emotional moment. The fact that six of Ecuador's Jaguar aircraft had first taken to the sky in the hands of this very capable pilot is now perhaps lost but for Eric, with over 14,000 hours in his logbook, 327's journey is perhaps one of the most significant.

Above: Those aircraft not loaned out for display currently reside in revetments at the Taura base serving effectively in a decoy capacity.

Left: Ecuador undertook some modification of its own to the defensive aid suite of the Jaguar with the addition of chaff/flare dispensers. These were placed onto the underwing pylons.

One Jaguar to enter
the hall of fame was
XZ118. Purchased from
Everett Aerospace,
which in turn had
acquired it from RAF
surplus stocks, artist
Fiona Banner turned it
into a highly polished
example in her Tate
Modern exhibition.
Later it was sold to the
Slimelight nightclub
in Islington, London
but later disposed of
as scrap.

Aviation Art – Apparently

I AM NOT PARTICULARLY an art lover, although I do boast of the late Miles Birkett Foster being a relation. That said I was intrigued by the Fiona Banner exhibition being staged at London's Tate Britain Art Gallery between June 2010 and January 2011.

Banner is better known for her 'wordscapes' or written transcriptions of the frame-by-frame action of some of Hollywood's famous war movies; however, the emblem of the fighter aircraft had apparently long fascinated her. It seems that her compulsion to grasp the uncomfortable resonances of these war-like machines had produced for her a growing archive of material; from pencil drawings to newspaper cuttings and 'airfix' model collections the modesty of her works were seen to contrast with the heroic connotations of her subjects.

According to the Tate's curator of contemporary British art, by placing decommissioned fighter planes in the incongruous setting of the Duveen Galleries Banner represented the opposite of language when communication fails.

Apparently the exhibition brought body and machine into close proximity, exploring the tension between the intellectual perception of the fighter aircraft and the physical experience of the object.

Banner suspended a decommissioned former Royal Navy Sea Harrier FA.2, thought to be ZE695, from the ceiling of the Duveen Galleries transforming it into a captive bird. The highly polished Sepecat Jaguar GR.1 XZ118 lying belly up on the floor is supposed to suggest the posture of a submissive animal.

In the description of the art at the Tate, Fiona Banner herself said:

I remember long sublime walks in the Welsh mountains with my father, when suddenly a fighter plane would rip through the sky, and shatter everything, it was so exciting, loud and overwhelming, it would literally take our breath away. The sound would arrive from nowhere, all you would see was the shadow and then it was gone.

That I can come to terms with and fully appreciate. As for this being art – well, that I find a little less easy to understand. To cap this Banner subsequently took the carcass of a decommissioned Panavia Tornado F.3 fighter acquired from a scrapyard in Seaham and melted the alloys down. She then had them recast into a bell and named it Project ZE728, taken from the aircraft's former identity.

The bell was hung in a frame and placed on the Hillgate Quay in Gateshead, not far from Millennium Bridge, for all to ring. On display from mid July to early September 2010 it was, when I visited the structure, sat forlorn and forgotten on a bit of disused Tyne quayside without any passing reference to what it represented. The only thing that perhaps surprised me was that given its location, it wasn't covered in graffiti!

While some may consider this art, for me they are just yesterday's aviation hardware used effectively and paid for by the taxpayer. I just hope we haven't paid again to turn them into something different.

Prototype RAF Jaguar XW563 was once displayed at the main gate at RAF Coltishall. Closure of the base in 2006 saw the airframe being donated to the Norfolk County Hall where it still resides today.

RAF JAGUAR INDIVIDUAL AIRCRAFT HISTORY

BAC/BAE Systems-Produced Jaguar Aircraft – Abridged Histories

XW560

S06 was rolled out on 18 August 1969 with its first flight (F/F) on 12 October 1969 (J.L. Dell) and used in handling trials, flutter and structural testing. It was written off (W/O) on 11 August 1972 due to a rear-end ground fire at Boscombe Down and after return to Warton withdrawn from use (WFU). The aircraft was used as static test aircraft for gun trials. The centre fuselage went to Lossiemouth for instructional duties by September 1973 before relocating to the JMU at Abingdon by October 1977, finally moving to Coltishall in June 1979 before disposal. Cockpit preserved at Boscombe Down until at least 2010 when the collection was relocated to Old Sarum where it still resides.

XW563

S07 was rolled out on 25 March 1970. Its F/F was on 12 June 1970 (J.L. Dell) and was used as a trials aircraft with the Elliot digital inertial NAVWASS. On flight 601 it undertook its F/F with 'Magic'. The jet carried missiles on overwing pylons. At completion of trials the aircraft was delivered to RAF Bruggen for instructional duties on 26 January 1978. Allocated maintenance serial 8563M and following a period with No. 431 Maintenance Unit (MU), the airframe was mounted as gate guardian sporting the spurious serial 'XX822' and coded 'AA' in No. 14 Squadron markings as a memorial to the loss of that actual aircraft on 2 July 1976 and the first fatality involving the Jaguar aircraft. After the closure of RAF Bruggen the airframe was relocated to RAF Coltishall, Norfolk where it served in the same role. Upon the closure of Coltishall in 2006 the aircraft found a new home at the Norfolk County Hall where it still resides.

XW566

B08 F/F on 30 August 1971 (P. Millett) and differed from S07/S08 as the airframe was made up of predominantly production parts enabling it to be tested towards production standard. Testing was undertaken at both Warton and Boscombe Down before transfer to the RAE at Farnborough on 3 February 1982 after ten and a half years at Warton and 718 flights. Last flight (L/F) was on 17 June 1985 and WFU shortly afterwards. It is now preserved at Farnborough.

XX108

S1 F/F 1 October 1972 (T.M.S. Ferguson), 27 April 1973 D/D (date delivered) at Boscombe Down for testing by 'A' Squadron. The jet alternated between A&AEE and BAC and was involved in spinning trials between 1977 and 1979 followed by engine development work. It was bailed back to the company for the 1979 Paris Salon as G-27-313 where it suffered a nose wheel collapse during a short-field take-off/landing demonstration. It was taken by road to the JMU at RAF Abingdon where a new nose section was fitted, it returned to Warton on 7 August 1980. While undergoing overhaul with No. 19 MU at RAF St Athan in February 1994 the jet received a 'Children in Need' inscription.

The first production Jaguar GR.1, XX108, was retained by the parent company at its Warton facility where it undertook a multitude of development testing. Its final role was that of Rolls-Royce Adour 106 engine upgrade. It is seen here on its penultimate flight before retirement and delivery to the Imperial War Museum at Duxford.

It was upgraded to GR.1B standard at St Athan in mid 1996 and returned to Warton in 2000 to undertake Adour 106 flight trials before making its last flight back to St Athan on 28 May 2002. Presented to the Imperial War Museum (IWM) it was placed on-charge of the RAF Museum at RAF Cosford on 28 October 2003 before finally relocating to the IWM at Duxford in 2005.

XX109

S2 F/F 16 November 1972 (P. Millett), D/D on 1 May 1973 at Boscombe Down for use by 'A' Squadron, A&AEE. It went to Warton in March 1979 where it undertook motorway landing/take-off trials on an unopened stretch of the M55 near Blackpool over the period 26–27 April 1979. It was retained for engine development work with the aircraft retired in 1986 and, with Squadron Leader Mike Rondot as pilot, was delivered to RAF Coltishall on 21 October 1986 for use as a weapon load training instructional airframe and given the maintenance serial 8918M. It received the code 'US' in 1996 and it was then repainted in a desert-pink ARTF colour scheme. By May 1998 it was finally retired from use and presented to the City of Norwich Museum on 1 September 2004 where it still resides.

XX110

S3 F/F 1 March 1973 (J.J. Cockburn) and D/D on 112th flight to A&AEE at Boscombe Down on 26 April 1974. Flown to No. 60MU RAF Leconfield on 26 April 1976 the aircraft was retrofitted with the modified nose section containing the laser ranger and delivered to No. 6 Squadron the following month. Receiving the individual code of 'EP' it served with the squadron until 24 July 1985 when it was dispatched to RAF Shawbury for storage. Allocated the maintenance serial 8955M it was delivered to No. 2 (now No. 1) School of Technical Training (No. 2 SoTT) at RAF Cosford where it resides today.

XX111

S4 F/F 17 April 1973 (D. Eagles) and D/D to RAF Lossiemouth 30 May 1973 for use by No. 226 Operational Conversion Unit (No. 226 OCU), receiving the individual code '01'. It served with the unit until 16 November 1976 when it was flown to the JMU for fitment of the modified nose section. This was completed early in 1977 and the aircraft was placed into operational store on 6 May 1977. It was released from store and flown to Warton on 16 October 1979 by Eric Bucklow as G-27-314 as part of the IAF loan deal. It was upgraded to Jaguar International configuration with its F/F after upgrade on 21 December 1979 when the jet was delivered to the IAF as JI 011 on 13 February 1980. XX111 was lost on operations in 10 April 1982.

XX112

S5 F/F on 2 May 1973 (T.M.S. Ferguson) and delivered to Boscombe Down on 17 September 1973 for use by 'A' Squadron A&AEE. It was sent to JMU store by September 1978 and was reissued to No. 6 Squadron on 18 October 1979. Sporting a white diamond marking on the tail and upper-wing surface in October 1980 the jet was upgraded to GR.1A standard at the JMU in early 1985. The jet returned to No. 6 Squadron on 25 January 1985 receiving the individual code of 'EA'. Recoded 'EC' by May 1990 the aircraft received the ARTF desert-pink scheme for participation in Operation Granby in August 1990. Replaced in theatre it returned to Coltishall and regained its 'EC' code. Dispatched to St Athan for upgrade to Jaguar 96 configuration on 4 March 1997 it returned to the squadron as 'EA' on 23 February 1998. Redesignated Jaguar GR.3 it received the ARTF grey scheme for overseas operations in February 2003 before once again being dispatched for upgrade to GR.3A configuration. In October 2003 it received No. 6 Squadron 60th-anniversary markings. It was with No. 19 MU at RAF St Athan in December 2004 before reissue to No. 6 Squadron as 'EA' in October 2005, where it served until retirement in 2007. It was flown to RAF Cosford for instructional duties where it remains today.

XX113

S6 F/F 31 May 1973 (P. Ginger) and was delivered to Boscombe Down on 18 October 1973 for use by 'A' Squadron A&AEE. Following overhaul at No. 60 MU in 1975 it was delivered to No. 226 OCU on 22 December 1975 taking up the individual code of '09'. Repainted in all-over wraparound colours at No. 5 MU RAF Kemble in August 1976 it returned to the unit until lost in a crash on 17 July 1981 near Malvern whilst on a post-overhaul test flight from the JMU at RAF Abingdon.

XX114

S7 F/F 5 July 1973 (P. Ginger) and delivered to RAF Lossiemouth on 13 September 1973, after being used at Warton on RAF conversion training, taking the individual code '02' with No. 226 OCU. It was repainted in wraparound camouflage at No. 5 MU RAF Kemble during April 1976. It was lost on take-off from RAF Lossiemouth whilst operating with No. 226 OCU on 19 September 1983 with the pilot

successfully ejecting. The remains were passed to JMU with wings being noted in March 1984. The wreck was eventually disposed of to Park Aviation, Faygate, Sussex and was still reported extant in March 2005.

XX115

S8 F/F 16 August 1973 (J.J. Cockburn) and D/D to RAF Lossiemouth 13 September 1973 becoming code '03' with No. 226 OCU. This was the first aircraft to be fitted with the RWR on the fin. Passed into operational store with JMU on 27 January 1978 until resurrected for use in the Indian loan deal, returning to Warton as G-27-315 on 10 June 1979. Upgraded to Jaguar International standard it was delivered to India as JI 005 on 11 December 1979. Following delivery of new aircraft to the IAF the jet was flown back to RAF St Athan on 23 July 1982 before transferring to No. 27 MU at RAF Shawbury for storage. Allocated maintenance serial 8821M it was issued to No. 1 SoTT at RAF Halton in August 1984, although the centre fuselage was noted with the JMU just prior to this. This section was eventually issued to No. 2 SoTT at RAF Cosford where it is believed to have been scrapped in 2007.

XX116

S9 rolled out 22 August 1973 and F/F 10 September 1973 (T. Ferguson). D/D to RAF Lossiemouth 2 October 1973 for use by No. 226 OCU as individual code '04'. It was repainted into wraparound camouflage at No. 5 MU RAF Kemble in October 1976 and passed into the JMU operational store on 22 February 1978. Identified as part of the IAF loan deal it was flown back to Warton as G-27-316 on 2 August 1979 for upgrade to Jaguar International standard before being delivered to India as

JI 008. It returned to the UK on 19 April 1984 direct to Warton for storage. Upgraded to GR.1A standard the aircraft was reissued to No. 6 Squadron as 'EE' before being transferred to No. 226 OCU on 9 December 1986 to become code '02'. After No. 226 OCU became No. 16 (Reserve) Squadron the jet received an all-over black colour scheme with a yellow 'Saint' emblem on the tail for the 1993 air-show season. Allocated individual code 'B' it received the new standard all-over grey colour scheme by May 1997 when it was transferred to No. 6 Squadron as aircraft 'EO'.

The jet became the second Jaguar 97 trials aircraft in January 1999 although, retaining its nominal No. 6 Squadron allocation, it alternated between Defence Evaluation and Research Agency (DERA), the manufacturer and the front line until it was retired and WFU at St Athan in March 2005. Later issued to the Fire Services Central Training Establishment (FSCTE) at Manston by April 2006 and was still reported as current in April 2014.

XX117

S10 F/F 8 October 1973 (D. Eagles) and D/D to RAF Lossiemouth 31 October 1973 where it took up the individual code '05' with No. 226 OCU. Delivered to No. 60 MU for nose retrofit in April 1975 it was then issued to No. 6 Squadron on 29 April 1976. After a short period at No. 5 MU RAF Kemble to receive the wraparound all-over camouflage the aircraft alternated its time between the front line and trials work at Boscombe Down with the A&AEE. Passed into operational store with the JMU on 25 March 1977, it was identified for the Indian loan deal. Returned to Warton as G-27-317 on 15 June 1979. After upgrade to Jaguar International the aircraft was delivered to India as JI 004 on 14 October 1979, returning to the UK on 24 February 1984 to Warton where it was upgraded to GR.1A standard. Reissued to No. 54 Squadron as 'GG' by November 1984 it moved onto No. 226 OCU by March 1986 as '06'. Transferred into short-term store with No. 27 MU in October 1990 it was reassigned to the RAE at Farnborough on 25 January 1991 although retained its former owner's marks.

Upgraded later to Jaguar 96 configuration and used by the Strike Attack Operational Evaluation Unit (SAOEU) at Boscombe Down the jet returned to St Athan for overhaul in early 1998 before reissue to No. 6 Squadron at Coltishall where it became 'EB'. It was transferred to No. 16 Squadron as 'A' on 17 December 1998 before being recoded 'PA' on the units relocation to RAF Coltishall. Upgraded to GR.3A in 2001 it remained with No. 16 Squadron receiving the unit's special 90th-anniversary scheme in January 2005. At the demise of the squadron in the following March it was assigned the code 'ES' with No. 6 Squadron, which was applied to the nose wheel door (NWD) but the service was short-lived and the aircraft was flown to St Athan on 1 July 2005 where it was WFU. It was reassigned as a ground instructional airframe with No. 1 SoTT at RAF Cosford becoming the first of many GR.3A versions to enter the technical training role.

XX118

S11 F/F 24 October 1973 (J. Preece) and D/D RAF Lossiemouth for No. 226 OCU 19 November 1973 where it became '06'. Following overhaul at No. 60 MU the jet was dispatched to No. 5 MU for repainting in the wraparound all-over camouflage scheme in March 1976. Following this it was issued to No. 6 Squadron at RAF

Coltishall on 6 May 1976 before dispatch to the JMU for laser nose and RWR retrofit. After returning to No. 6 Squadron it passed into short-term operational store with the JMU by 16 January 1978. Identified for the Indian loan deal it was flown to Warton as G-27-318 on 13 February 1980 for upgrade to Jaguar International standard. Delivered to India as JI 008 on 11 December 1979 it later returned to the UK on 25 May 1982, initially to St Athan then into store with No. 27 MU at RAF Shawbury by December 1983. Allocated to instructional use with maintenance serial 8815M it departed Shawbury on 10 April 1984 ostensibly to Abingdon for battle-damage repair training. It was noted in May 1984 en route to the Proof and Experimental Establishment (PEE) Foulness Island before returning to the JMU by November 1984. It was then passed to No. 1 SoTT at RAF Halton on 23 August 1985 but on closure of that facility it returned to Abingdon where the fuselage was noted dumped in February 1992.

XX119

S12 F/F 5 November 1973 (P. Ginger) and D/D to RAF Lossiemouth 17 December 1973 for No. 226 OCU as individual code '07'. Following overhaul at No. 60 MU it was reassigned to No. 54 Squadron by 1 September 1975. Repainted into wraparound all-over camouflage at No. 5 MU Kemble in August 1976 it returned to No. 54 Squadron and when individual code letters were assigned at RAF Coltishall it became 'GC'. Loaned to the A&AEE during 1982 it had by May 1986 been reassigned to No. 226 OCU again as code '01'. Allocated to ground training shortly afterwards and assigned the maintenance serial 8898M it never took up this role instead remaining in service with No. 226

OCU and was one of the first aircraft to receive the units new tartan fin marking in 1994. Becoming 'A' with No. 16 (Reserve) Squadron when the OCU took over this mantle it was later, following overhaul, assigned the code letter 'E' before receiving the new grey colour scheme in February 1997. It was reassigned to No. 54 squadron as 'GD' although loaned to DERA in April 1998 and was upgraded to Jaguar 96 configuration. Converted to Jaguar 97 by early 2000 it was redesignated GR.3A two years later remaining as 'GD' until the demise of No. 54 Squadron in March 2005. Allocated the code 'EB' with No. 6 Squadron in the subsequent reshuffle where it served until retirement in 2007. There after it joined the growing fleet of instructional airframes at RAF Cosford.

XX120

S13 F/F 23 November 1973 (E. Bucklow) and D/D to RAF Lossiemouth for use by No. 226 OCU as code '08'. Following overhaul at No. 60 MU and subsequent laser nose/RWR retrofit it was reassigned to No. 54 Squadron and lost in a crash off Samsoe Island, Denmark during Exercise Teamwork 76 on 17 September 1976.

XX121

S14 F/F 21 December 1973 (P. Ginger) and delivered to RAF Lossiemouth on 1 February 1974 for No. 226 OCU as code '09'. This was the first aircraft to be fitted with the in-flight refuelling probe and was reassigned to No. 54 Squadron in July 1974. Retrofitted with laser nose and RWR at No. 60 MU between 6 August 1975 and 11 November 1975 the jet was subsequently coded 'GB' with the squadron. Reassigned to No. 6 Squadron as 'EQ' by July 1984 it was passed into long-term store at No. 27 MU RAF Shawbury on 12 November 1984. Taken from store and transferred to Warton in expectation of a follow-on order from the Ecuadorian Air Force, when this failed to materialise it was returned to Shawbury in July 1993. Finally disposed of post-1994 and sold to Park Aviation Supply at Charlwood in June 1998, where it was noted as late as July 2012. It was then sold to a private collector at Thorpe Wood, Selby, North Yorkshire in February 2015.

XX122

S15 F/F 11 January 1974 (E. Bucklow) and D/D to RAF Lossiemouth 1 February 1974 for No. 226 OCU as code '10'. Following overhaul and retrofit at No. 60 MU the aircraft was reassigned to No. 54 Squadron on 13 October 1975 subsequently taking up the code 'GA' on 26 January 1981. It was later lost in an accident on 2 April 1982 when the aircraft crashed into the Wash off Heacham. The remains were initially taken to the JMU at RAF Abingdon before transfer to the Air Investigations Branch (AIB) at Farnborough on 13 April 1982 where they remained until at least March 1986.

XX136

B1 F/F 28 March 1973 (J. Cockburn/R. Stock). Flown by Joint Chief of the Air Staff Sir Dennis Smallwood on 23 May 1973 and delivered to A&AEE at Boscombe Down on 1 June 1973 it was lost in an accident near Winterbourne Gunner on 22 November 1974.

XX137

B2 F/F 26 June 1973 (P. Ginger/R. Kenward). It was evaluated by Kuwaiti pilot L. Duaij on 22 August 1973 and by Ecuadorean pilots Colonel Pazmino and Colonel Mora on 30 August 1973.

The third production RAF two-seat Jaguar XX138 saw limited service within the RAF. It served for a short period with No. 226 OCU before being loaned to India in 1979 as JI001. It was then sold on to Oman without returning to RAF charge, becoming No. 200 in RAFO service and one of the last Jaguars flying outside India.

It was then used for RAF IP training between 4 September 1973 and 26 September 1973. D/D to Lossiemouth 4 October 1973 it was the first aircraft for No. 226 OCU coded 'A'. Returning to Warton on 5 February 1975 as crew ferry for S45 the one engine flamed out on approach, and it was retained for investigation. It unfortunately crashed into Moray Firth on 6 February 1976. The wreck was recovered and dispatched to JMU on 24 June 1976 before later transferring to the AWRE (Atomic Weapons Research Establishment) at the PEE Foulness Island where it was still extant in December 1981. Some remains found in the AIB compound at Farnborough in March 1982 with the remainder being sold to Park Aviation Supply, Faygate, Sussex where they were still noted as being extant in 1991.

XX138

B3 F/F 10 October 1973 (J.J. Lee/J. Preece) and D/D to RAF Lossiemouth for No. 226 OCU with individual aircraft code 'B'. Overhauled at No. 60 MU in early 1976 it was dispatched to Warton from Lossiemouth as G-27-319 on 18 December 1978 as part of Indian loan deal. Flown to India as JI 001 on 23 July 1979. At the end of the loan it was sold to Oman as aircraft serial 200 in January 1982 but flown to UK to cure a persistent fuel leak. It arrived at JMU on 15 September 1983 returning to Oman on 13 December 1983.

XX139

B4 F/F 5 December 1973 (J. Cockburn/S. Boston) and D/D to RAF Lossiemouth 3 January 1974 for No. 226 OCU and individual code letter 'C'. Reassigned to No. 6 Squadron by October 1984

After a varied front-line career XX141 seen here joined the Airframe Maintenance Instruction Flight at RAF Cranwell, gaining the maintenance serial 9297M. The flight relocated to RAF Cosford in 2013, taking their assigned airframes with them.

No. 226 OCU as individual code 'E'. Converted to Jaguar T.2A configuration by February 1985 it was then issued to No. 6 Squadron as 'ET'. It returned to No. 226 OCU as 'Z' post-1989 becoming No. 16 (Reserve) Squadron 'Z' when the unit changed designation by March 1994. By July 1996 it had returned to No. 6 Squadron as 'EV' before being retired and becoming a ground-maintenance trainer with the 'Aircraft Maintenance Instruction Flight' at RAF Cranwell with maintenance serial 9297M. When the school relocated to RAF Cosford in August 2006 so with it went its Jaguar airframes, including XX141.

XX142

B7 F/F 29 March 1974 (J. Preece/A. Love) and D/D to RAF Lossiemouth 8 May 1974 for use by No. 226 OCU as individual code 'G'. Aircraft later crashed 10 miles north of Lossiemouth on 22 June 1979 with the loss of both crew. Remains noted with the AIB at Farnborough but later scrapped.

XX143

B8 F/F 14 March 1974 (J. Preece/E. Bucklow) D/D to RAF Lossiemouth 18 April 1974 for use by No. 226 OCU as individual code 'F'. At Cat it suffered three bird strikes on 29 May 1975, which caused major damage. The aircraft recovered but did not fly again until 30 March 1977. It was later identified for the Indian loan deal and was delivered from Lossiemouth to Warton on 21 December 1978 as G-27-321. The jet departed for India as JI 002 on 14 October 1979, returning to the UK at RAF Abingdon on 9 September 1982. After a period in store and then overhaul with the JMU it was reissued to No. 226 OCU as 'B' on 17 October 1983 before transfer to No. 54 Squadron in August 1987,

as 'ES' it was upgraded to Jaguar T.2A standard in mid 1985 and reissued to No. 226 OCU taking up its old code. Recoded 'T' by March 1994 it was loaned to the DTEO in September 1997 and then following the T.4 upgrade it was transferred back to No. 16 (Reserve) Squadron as 'T' by January 2000. On 12 April 2005 it was flown from RAF Coltishall to St Athan for spares recovery. It was sold to Everett Aerospace at Sproughton on 27 October 2005 and was noted as current in April 2014.

XX140

B5 F/F 21 December 1973 (D. Eagles/R. Kenward) and D/D to RAF Lossiemouth 29 January 1974 for No. 226 OCU where it took the individual code letter 'D'. It was then transferred to No. 54 Squadron in July 1974 and then back to No. 226

OCU as 'D' again until retired to Shawbury on 4 July 1985. Allocated the maintenance serial 9008M at No. 2 SoTT at RAF Cosford the jet was subsequently disposed of, with the hulk passing into the hands of Park Aviation Supply at Faygate, Sussex in May 1999. The remains were reported current as late as January 2006 before going to Conifer Metals in June 2006. Some confusion then appears, as the airframe once again was reported at Charlwood in July 2012 but by February 2015 it had passed into the hands of a private collector at Thorpe Wood, Selby, North Yorkshire.

XX141

B6 F/F 25 January 1974 (P. Ginger/R. Stock). Evaluated by Belgian AF on 20 February 1974 and D/D to RAF Lossiemouth 13 March 1974 for becoming code 'GS' with the unit. Aircraft passed into short-term store with No. 27 MU at RAF Shawbury in late 1992 before being transferred to St Athan to upgrade to Jaguar T.2B standard. However, work was not completed due to limited airframe-fatigue life. It returned to service with No. 16 (Reserve) Squadron as code 'X', still as a Jaguar T.2A, but was lost in a crash in the Moray Firth on 18 September 1976 shortly after take-off from RAF Lossiemouth. The pilot ejected safely and the airframe was recovered by Chinook HC.2 ZA681 'ED' of No. 7 Squadron on 25 September 1996. The remains were sold to Park Aviation Supply at Faygate, Sussex by March 1998.

XX144

B9 F/F 11 July 1974 (J. Preece/D. Wilkinson) and D/D to RAF Lossiemouth 11 July 1974 for No. 226 OCU code 'K'. It suffered an undercarriage collapse on 9 September 1974 and was returned to Warton for repairs on 12 January 1975. Rebuild completed with F/F 1 October 1976 and aircraft was issued to No. 54 Squadron on 2 November 1976. Transferred to No. 6 Squadron as 'ET' by February 1981 it had been upgraded to T.2A configuration at the JMU during March 1985. It was returned to No. 6 Squadron strength until transferred to No. 226 OCU in August 1985 becoming code 'I'. Recoded 'U' with No. 16 (Reserve) Squadron in May 1994 the aircraft was flown to RAF Shawbury for long-term store in early 2000 where it remains today, although its disposal is imminent having been put up for it by tender DSAT (defence system approach to training) 3146 on 26 May 2005 and destined for Dick Everett Aero, Sproughton, Suffolk, arriving by October 2005; it still resided there in April 2014.

Not all Jaguar airframes had particularly happy endings. XX145, depicted here in the standard raspberry-ripple colours of the Royal Aircraft Establishment, is seen stripped of usable parts and in use for crash-rescue training at RAF Cranwell. It was eventually saved from destruction by a private collector and is now stored at Bruntingthorpe.

XX145

B10 F/F 24 May 1974 (E. Bucklow/A. Begg) and D/D to RAF Lossiemouth 14 June 1974 for use by No. 226 OCU as code 'H'. The jet was transferred to the Empire Test Pilots' School on 3 February 1984 as a replacement for XX915 where it received its 'corporate' red, white and blue colour scheme in mid 1989. Remained on strength until at least July 2005, being withdrawn shortly afterwards. After spares recovery the airframe was given to the fire school at RAF Cranwell by April 2010 before being acquired for possible preservation at Bruntingthorpe where it is believed to still reside.

XX146

B11 F/F 24 May 1974 (J. Cockburn/R. Stock) and D/D to RAF Lossiemouth 10 July 1974 for use by No. 226 OCU as individual code 'J'. It was transferred to RAF Coltishall post overhaul at No. 60 MU on 29 October 1976 eventually taking up No. 6 Squadron markings. Returned to Lossiemouth as 'J' for a short period during 1980–81, it later returned to Coltishall on 2 April 1981 becoming No. 6 Squadron 'S'. The aircraft was transferred to No. 41 Squadron retaining the same code in late 1983 before passing on No. 54 Squadron as 'GS' in July 1984. It suffered an engine failure on take-off from Coltishall on 30 August 1984 but was recovered after pilot jettisoned all external stores. It passed into short-term store with No. 27 MU between 1987 and 1991 before returning to Coltishall and being assigned to No. 41 Squadron as 'Y'. The jet was reassigned to No. 16 (Reserve) Squadron as 'J' again in February 1993 before being recoded 'X' by the following March. It was upgraded to Jaguar T.2B configuration and allocated to No. 54 Squadron as 'GT', although retaining its former marks until return from a loan period between December 1995 and March 1996 with the SAOEU when the new insignia was applied. The aircraft went to St Athan in April 1999 for modification to T.4, returning to No. 54 Squadron in November 2000. The jet was finally retired on 7 March 2005 when it was flown to St Athan for spares recovery. Acquired by Dick Everett it had arrived at Sproughton by December 2005 and was last noted in April 2014.

XX147

B12 F/F 2 July 1974 (E. Bucklow/R. Stock) and D/D to RAF Lossiemouth 20 August 1974 for No. 226 OCU as code 'L'. It was reassigned to No. 2 Squadron as 'II' on 30 June 1976 and later transferred to No. 17 Squadron as 'BY'. It was lost in a crash on 26 March 1979 at Südlohn, Borken, West Germany following a bird strike; both crew ejected safely.

XX148

B13 F/F 13 August 1974 (J.J. Lee/R.T. Taylor) and flown by RSAF pilots on evaluation, including Commander-in-Chief Lieutenant General Al-Zuhair. It was delivered to RAF Lossiemouth on 13 September 1974 for use by No. 226 OCU as code 'M'. It crashed at Whittingham with the loss of both crew on 29 July 1977.

XX149

B14 F/F 27 August 1974 (T. Ferguson/R.T. Taylor) and used in RSAF evaluation. D/D to RAF Lossiemouth 20 September 1974 for use by No. 226 OCU as individual code 'N'. The aircraft crashed on 27 April 1978 at Cullen, Banff whilst en route from RAF Coltishall to RAF Lossiemouth.

XX150

B15 F/F 30 September 1974 (A. Love/R. Woollett) and D/D to RAF Lossiemouth 23 October 1974

for use by No. 6 Squadron that was forming at the time. It went to Coltishall on 6 November 1974 and following overhaul with No. 60 MU was reassigned to No. 20 Squadron and then No. 31 Squadron where it took the code 'DY'. It transferred on 13 October 1982 to No. 14 Squadron as 'AZ' where it stayed with the unit for a year before once again serving with No. 31 Squadron, this time as 'DZ'. Returned to No. 14 Squadron as 'AX' by October 1984; it remained with the unit until it converted to Tornado. It was flown to No. 27 MU RAF Shawbury for short-term store in November 1985 and after overhaul at the JMU it was assigned to No. 226 OCU as code 'W' by June 1989. The aircraft suffered an undercarriage collapse at Lossiemouth on 22 November 1990. Following an overhaul at St Athan in January 1993 it was assigned to No. 16 (Reserve) Squadron as 'W' by March 1994. An upgrade to T.4 followed and after a period of loan with DERA in late 1999 and relocation to RAF Coltishall it was recoded 'PW'. It transferred to No. 41 Squadron as 'FY' in March 2005 following the unit's disbandment. It was WFU at St Athan in March 2006 and was acquired for possible preservation, arriving at the former RAF Bentwaters for store on 9 August 2006. It was last noted in September 2011.

XX719

S16 F/F 31 January 1974 (D. Eagles) and D/D to RAF Lossiemouth 4 March 1974 for No. 226 OCU with individual code '11'. It was reassigned to No. 54 Squadron on July 1974 and eventually coded 'GD' by February 1981 when that station adopted individual code letters. It transferred to No. 6 Squadron as 'EB' by April 1985 later becoming 'EQ' and finally 'EE'. Received the ARTF desert-pink colour scheme for Operation Granby in August 1990 but was replaced in

theatre before war started. It was returned to normal scheme and code 'EE' but later sold to Oman following Jaguar 96 upgrade including TIALD integration. Became serial 226 and was delivered 10 August 1998.

XX720

S17 F/F 16 April 1974 (T. Ferguson) and D/D to Boscombe Down 8 May 1974 for 'A' Squadron A&AEE following preparation for tropical/arctic trials in USA. The jet flew to CFB Goose Bay with Wing Commander M. Adams on 9 July 1974, returning to Warton on 13 November 1975 suitably emblazoned with various badges on the fin – including a maple leaf, a Fox's polar bear and a red 'X' on the ECM pod – having completed nearly 200 flights. Following service-acceptance trials it was flown to JMU and placed in short-term store on 21 February 1977. Identified as a candidate for the Indian loan deal it was flown to Warton as G-27-319 on 22 May 1979. Following upgrade to Jaguar International standard it was delivered to India on 23 July 1979 as JI 003 by Chris Yeo via Toulouse, Brindisi, Larnaca, Baghdad, Seeb and Jamnagar, arriving at Ambala after 11 hours airborne.

It was returned to the UK and Warton on 24 February 1984 to be brought up to GR.1A standard. Reissued to No. 54 Squadron as 'GQ' on 21 March 1985 but, following overhaul at JMU in February 1988, loaned to A&AEE before returning to Coltishall on 3 May 1988 for No. 6 Squadron and assigned code 'EN'. It received ARTF desert-pink colour scheme as spare aircraft for Operation Granby, it then resumed normal scheme as 'EN' then placed in short-term store at RAF Shawbury between mid 1992 and late 1995. Upgraded at St Athan to GR.1A (T) standard and TIALD capable.

PF XX723, one of the last RAF Jaguars in service. The jet moved to RAF Coningsby following the disbandment of No. 41 Squadron and saw limited service with No. 6 Squadron. It is captured here over Lincolnshire during the 2006 Queen's birthday fly-past practice.

Upon completion it was assigned to No. 54 Squadron as 'GB' sporting the new grey colour scheme. It was upgraded again as Jaguar 96 before final modification to GR.3A at St Athan in early 2001, returning to No. 54 Squadron upon completion. The aircraft received an arctic ARTF scheme for Exercise Snow Goose at Bardufoss in January 2005 and transferred to No. 41 Squadron in March 2005 as 'FL'. It was passed into store at St Athan on 20 May 2005 until at least March 2006. The jet was sold to Everett Aerospace by January 2007 and was still current in April 2014.

XX721

S18 F/F 6 February 1974 (E. Bucklow) and D/D to RAF Lossiemouth 28 February 1974 as first-production GR.1 for No. 54 Squadron, although wore the number eleven on the NWD as part of No. 226 OCU before squadron stood up. Eventually coded 'GE' after squadron moved to RAF Coltishall but lost in a crash on 12 June 1983 near to Hahn whilst on a NATO (North Atlantic Treaty Organisation) exchange visit to the 313th Tactical Fighter Squadron (TFS).

XX722

S19 F/F 28 February 1974 (J. Preece) and D/D to RAF Lossiemouth 20 March 1974 for

No. 54 Squadron although carried code '13' of No. 226 OCU until squadron officially formed. Upon relocation to RAF Coltishall took up the code 'GF' in February 1981 but reassigned to No. 6 Squadron by May 1984, becoming 'EF' in the process. It was placed in store at RAF Shawbury on 22 January 1985 but was transferred to Warton for possible resale to Ecuador. When that fell through the aircraft was returned to Shawbury in July 1993 until transfer to DARA at St Athan for battle-damage-repair training on 25 June 1997. Still current in March 2002 then transferred to the Aircraft Recovery and Recovery Flight until disposal in September 2005. The airframe is reported to have been scrapped by January 2006 although the nose section is thought to have survived with the school.

XX723

S20 F/F 19 March 1974 (E. Bucklow) and D/D RAF Lossiemouth 8 April 1974 for No. 54 Squadron although initially received code '14' as part of No. 226 OCU. The move to Coltishall saw code 'GG' assigned before transfer to No. 6 Squadron in late 1984 when it took the code 'EQ'. Transferred back to No. 226 OCU as '07' in March 1986, the aircraft spent a number of periods on loan with the Coltishall squadrons. It was recoded '05' in March 1988 and finally reassigned to No. 54 Squadron as 'GQ' at the beginning of 1992. The new grey colour scheme was applied in July 1996 along with upgrade to GR.1B followed by Jaguar 97 in late 1999. Loaned to DERA and redesignated GR.3A in November 1999 the jet received at least one application of ARTF grey for overseas deployment and remained with No. 54 Squadron until its demise when it was transferred to No. 41 Squadron as 'FF'.

Following disbandment the aircraft was transferred to No. 6 Squadron as 'EU' in April 2006. Placed into store at RAF Shawbury on 14 December 2006 and moved to RAF Cosford for instructional duties by August 2009 it was still current in November 2013.

XX724

S21 F/F 26 April 1974 (D. Eagles) and undertook AAR trials with A&AEE. D/D to RAF Lossiemouth 29 May 1974 for No. 54 Squadron although carried the code '15' during the No. 226 OCU work-up period. When the Coltishall squadrons adopted code letters the aircraft became 'GA' until it passed into long-term store at RAF Shawbury on 27 February 1989. Dispatched to St Athan on 13 April 1999 for overhaul it was returned to No. 54 Squadron on 2 April 2001, only to return to St Athan for GR.3A upgrade on 17 March 2003 from which it adopted the code 'GC'. Transferred to No. 6 Squadron in March 2005 it became 'EC' in the process. Remained with the unit until retirement in 2007, passing into the hands of RAF Cosford for instructional duties where it was still noted in November 2013.

XX725

S22 F/F 8 May 1974 (E. Bucklow) and D/D RAF Lossiemouth 30 May 1974 for No. 54 Squadron, temporarily adopting the code '16' for the No. 226 OCU work-up period. The jet went to JMU in January 1979 and was identified for Indian Air Force loan. It was ferried to Warton as G-27-325 on 20 September 1979. Following upgrade to Jaguar International configuration, it was flown to India on 13 February 1980 as JI 010. XX725 returned to the UK on 19 April 1984 and into short-term store at Warton. It was delivered back to Coltishall on 12 August 1985

as a GR.1A, becoming 'EL' of No. 6 Squadron. Repainted in the ARTF desert-pink colour scheme, and one of twelve aircraft to receive overwing missile rails and uprated engines, it was deployed to Thumrait and later Muharraq on 23 October 1990. Coded 'T' in theatre and named *Johnny Fartpants* upon its return to the UK on 13 March 1991 it carried forty-seven mission symbols. Reassigned to No. 54 Squadron as 'GU' it retained its ARTF scheme for a period as part of Operation Warden, but on repainting in October 1992 was inadvertently serialled XX729 on the portside, although this was rectified by 3 November 1992. Selected to receive stage three modifications, including fitment of Sky Guardian RWR and wiring for operation of TIALD it participated in Operation Deliberate Force in the new grey (baby blue) ARTF scheme.

In September 1995 it was noted wearing seven mission symbols comprising a blue lightning symbol beneath the cockpit on the port side. The normal scheme was reapplied in November 1995 with the designation having been unofficially altered to GR.1A (T) then GR.1B. Transferred to the SAOEU in October 1996 it returned to the squadron two years later, once again as 'GU'. Upgraded to GR.3 at St Athan during 1999 it alternated between No. 54 Squadron and the SAOEU for the next few years. Still as 'GU', it received the arctic ARTF finish in January 2005 for participation in Exercise Snow Goose at Bardufoss and upon its return was reassigned to No. 41 Squadron where it adopted the code 'GW'. It went to No. 6 Squadron as 'EE' by April 2006 remaining with the unit until disbandment in 2007. The jet was flown to RAF Cosford for instructional duties and it was still current in November 2013.

XX726

S23 F/F 7 May 1974 (P. Ginger) and D/D to RAF Lossiemouth for No. 6 Squadron. This was the first GR.1 to come off the production line already fitted with the redesigned nose section supporting the laser range finder. Ironically the nose was damaged by a forklift truck delaying its redeployment from Lossiemouth to Coltishall until 12 November 1974. Later assigned code 'EB' the aircraft was flown to No. 27 MU RAF Shawbury for storage during 1985, and then assigned to ground instructional duties at No. 1 SoTT at RAF Halton with maintenance serial 8947M. Upon closure of that facility it was transferred to RAF Cosford where it still resides.

XX727

S24 F/F 14 May 1974 (J.J. Lee) and D/D to RAF Lossiemouth 16 July 1974 for No. 6 Squadron. It received the code '21' during its period of work-up with No. 226 OCU and departed for Coltishall on 6 November 1974. It was transferred to No. 54 Squadron in November 1975 eventually adopting the code 'GJ' in January 1981. Returning to No. 6 Squadron as 'ER' in May 1984 it was then flown to RAF Shawbury for storage on 26 July 1984. It was assigned to ground instructional duties at No. 2 SoTT RAF Cosford as 8951M in 1988 where it still resides today.

XX728

S25 F/F 29 May 1974 (J. Cockburn) and D/D to RAF Lossiemouth 27 June 1974 for No. 226 OCU and adopting code '18'. During this period it undertook trials on the painting of the aircraft undersides to create an all-over wraparound camouflage. Reassigned to No. 6 Squadron on 28 October 1975 it was later identified as

Another former India loan aircraft, XX729, was to survive in RAF service to the bitter end. It is seen here starting its take-off run at RAF Coningsby.

a candidate for loan to India. It was flown to Warton as G-27-324 on 10 December 1978 and, following upgrade to Jaguar International standard, was delivered to India on 29 April 1980 as JI 009. It returned to St Athan (UK) on 23 July 1982 before transferring to JMU on 8 March 1983. Redelivered to No. 6 Squadron on 11 July 1983; as 'EH' it was later upgraded to GR.1A but was lost in a mid-air collision with XX731 on 7 October 1985 in the Hartside pass, Cumbria. Its remains were later noted in the Farnborough AIB compound in March 1986.

XX729

S26 F/F 3 July 1974 (J. Cockburn) and D/D to RAF Lossiemouth on 8 July 1974 for No. 226 OCU as code '19'. Reassigned to No. 6 Squadron on 1 September 1975 following overhaul at No. 60 MU it received the all-over wraparound

camouflage by March 1976. Identified as a candidate for loan to India it was flown to Warton as G-27-326 on 14 March 1979 and, following an upgrade to Jaguar International standard, was delivered to India on 19 April 1980 as JI 012. It was returned to St Athan on 25 May 1982 before being transferred to the JMU on 15 March 1983. Reassigned to No. 54 Squadron as 'GE' on 25 July 1983 it was transferred to No. 6 Squadron as 'EJ' by June 1984. It was upgraded to GR.1A in 1987 and reissued to No. 226 OCU eventually becoming code '07'. Back with No. 54 Squadron as 'GC' on 31 October 1988 it moved onto No. 6 Squadron again as 'EL', following repainting in the new permanent grey colour scheme on 15 March 1995. Conversion to GR.1B at St Athan in late 1995 was followed by a number of periods of loan to the SAOEU. Modified to

Jaguar 96 configuration at St Athan between 24 September 1998 and 25 March 1999 and then GR.3A in 2002 it remained on No. 6 Squadron strength as 'EL' until disbandment in 2007. It then went to RAF Cosford for instructional duties and was still current in November 2013.

XX730

S27 F/F 13 June 1974 (E. Bucklow) and D/D to RAF Lossiemouth 11 July 1974 for No. 226 OCU as code '20'. The aircraft went to No. 6 Squadron leaving Lossiemouth for Coltishall on 6 November 1974. Loaned to No. 54 Squadron for Red Flag deployment in 1980 was eventually to take up the code 'EC' by February 1981. The jet was flown to RAF Shawbury for storage in 1985 and assigned to ground instructional training in 1988. It was allocated maintenance serial 8952M with No. 2 SoTT at RAF Cosford until at least September 2005. By March 2010 it had been presented to the Polish Air Force Museum at Krakow where it is still current.

XX731

S28 F/F 3 July 1974 (J.J. Lee) and D/D to RAF Coltishall 23 August 1987 for No. 54 Squadron. It was coded 'GK' in February 1981 before transfer to No. 6 Squadron by April 1984. Coded initially 'EK' then following GR.1A upgrade 'ED' the jet was lost in a mid-air collision with XX728 over Hartside pass, Cumbria on 7 October 1985. Wreck later noted with AIB at Farnborough in March 1986.

XX732

S29 F/F 8 July 1974 (E. Bucklow) and D/D to RAF Lossiemouth 19 July 1974 for No. 54 Squadron. The aircraft received shark-mouth markings when attending the biannual 'Bulls Eye' competition at Husum airbase, West Germany

in October 1979 and was eventually coded 'GL' in February 1981. It was transferred to No. 6 Squadron as 'ED' by October 1983 then, following upgrade to GR.1A and overhaul at the JMU between 30 June 1985 and 25 September 1985, was reassigned to No. 226 OCU as '03' on 8 November 1985. It crashed on Stocks Hill in the Craik Forest, 11 miles south-west of Hawick on 27 November 1986 killing the USAF exchange pilot.

XX733

S30 F/F 17 July 1974 (J.J. Lee) and D/D to RAF Lossiemouth 21 August 1974 for No. 6 Squadron. It was noted sporting a white circle on its tail and upper-wing surfaces in October 1980 and assigned the code 'ED' in February 1981. It was delivered to Warton for FIN1064 installation in September 1983 followed by a period of loan with the A&AEE. The jet was reassigned to No. 54 Squadron as 'GL' then back to No. 6 Squadron again as 'EF'. It went to JMU in May 1990 for upgrade, including over-wing missile rails and Sky Guardian RWR, and the jet was resprayed in the ARTF desert-pink colour scheme for participation in Operation Granby departing for the Gulf on 23 October 1990. Whilst in theatre it received 'Fighter Pilot' nose art, the code 'R' on NWD and returned to the UK on 13 March 1991 sporting thirty-nine mission symbols. Returned to No. 6 Squadron marks as 'ER' by June 1991 it later had the ARTF grey scheme applied for participation in Operations Grapple and Warden. A new, permanent grey scheme was applied in June 1995 and aircraft redesignated GR.1B but it crashed on take-off from Coltishall on 23 January 1996 with the loss of the pilot. Remains stored on base until October 2000 until removed for scrap to Park Aviation

Supply, Faygate, Sussex surviving until 2007 when it was finally broken up and scrapped.

XX734

S31 F/F 5 August 1974 (E. Bucklow) and D/D RAF Lossiemouth 22 August 1974 for No. 6 Squadron. It went to Coltishall on 6 November 1974 and, following respray into the all-over wraparound camouflage at No. 5 MU Kemble in November 1976, it was identified as a candidate for loan to India. Flown to Warton as G-27-328 on 2 May 1979, following upgrade to Jaguar International configuration was delivered to India on 14 August 1980 as JI 014. It returned to St Athan on 11 February 1982 before transfer to store at RAF Shawbury. Allocated to ground instructional duties as 8816M it departed Shawbury on 10 April 1984, and by way of Farnborough, Abingdon it arrived at Coltishall for battle damage repair training (BDR) in November 1984. It was later disposed of to Park Aviation, Charlwood where it remained until at least August 2011. The nose section was passed onto the museum at Old Sarum in April 2014.

XX735

S32 F/F 15 August 1974 (P. Ginger) and D/D RAF Lossiemouth 13 September 1974 for No. 6 Squadron. It went to Coltishall on 6 November 1974; however, the aircraft was lost in a crash near Eggebek, West Germany on 15 September 1976 during 'Exercise Team Work 76'.

XX736

S33 F/F 27 August 1974 (J. Cockburn) and D/D RAF Lossiemouth 30 September 1974 for No. 226 OCU code '11'. It went to No. 6 Squadron on 22 December 1975 following overhaul at No. 60 MU and later to JMU. Identified as a candidate for loan to India it was flown to Warton as G-27-327 on 14 November 1979 and, following upgrade to Jaguar International standard, was delivered to India on 13 February 1980 as JI 013. Returning to Warton, UK on 24 February 1984 it was placed in store against potential overseas sales. It was then transferred to RAF Shawbury where it was to reside until assigned to ground instructional duties. The jet was allocated maintenance serial 9110M for BDR at RAF Coltishall where it was noted in February 1992. Nose and tail sections, along with an unidentified centre fuselage section from St Athan, were dispatched to BAE Systems at Brough for fatigue testing in late 1996, remaining there until the factory closed in February 2002. The nose section was acquired by Aero Venture (now South Yorkshire Aircraft Museum (SYAM)) in January 2007 where it still resides.

Delivered in 1974 XX738 gave the RAF over thirty years of continuous service. Seen here low down in the Machynlleth Loop of LFA7 doing what Jaguars do best.

XX737

S34 F/F 27 August 1974 (E. Bucklow) and D/D to RAF Lossiemouth 27 September 1974 for No. 226 OCU code '09'. It was reassigned to No. 54 Squadron following overhaul at No. 60 MU on 22 December 1975 but was later identified as a candidate for loan to India. The jet was flown to Warton as G-27-330 on 30 May 1979 and, following upgrade to Jaguar International standard, the aircraft was delivered to India on 14 August 1980 as JI 015. Returned to St Athan, UK on 25 May 1982 for short-term store. It went to JMU for overhaul in March 1983 before being reissued to No. 6 Squadron on 25 October 1983 as 'EN'. It was then transferred to No. 54 Squadron following an upgrade to GR.1A, becoming code 'GG', but put into short-term store at RAF Shawbury between 17 May 1989 and 6 November 1994; it later returned to No. 6 Squadron strength as 'EE'. It was upgraded to Jaguar 96 configuration at St Athan in mid 1997 and later to GR.3A in mid 2001. XX737 undertook operational duties abroad in February 2003 when the ARTF grey finish was applied. It was then with No. 6 Squadron as 'EE' until March 2006 when it was dispatched to St Athan, moving shortly after to store at the former RAF Bentwaters. It was acquired by Honeywell Aerospace, Phoenix, Arizona, USA in October 2008.

XX738

S35 F/F 9 September 1974 (E. Bucklow) and D/D to RAF Lossiemouth 27 September 1974 for No. 6 Squadron. It departed to RAF Coltishall on 6 November 1974 and again, following overhaul with No. 60 MU, was identified as a candidate for loan to India. It was later flown to Warton from Abingdon as G-27-329 on 14 March 1979 and, following upgrade to Jaguar International standard, was delivered to India on 13 February 1980 as JI 016. It was then returned to Abingdon, UK on 19 April 1984 and, following upgrade to GR.1A, was reissued to No. 54 Squadron as 'GJ' on 27 August 1984. However, it incurred a serious fuel transfer problem on take-off from RAF Chivenor on 11 August 1984, forcing the pilot to jettison all external stores into the River Taw before making an overweight landing. It was dispatched to JMU and later to short-term store at RAF Shawbury by November 1990 until at least December 1993. It later received stage three modifications as it was reissued to No. 6 Squadron on 12 December 1994, but transferred to No. 54 Squadron by February 1995 as 'GG'. The jet received a new grey colour scheme during overhaul at St Athan in early 1996 and was redesignated GR.1B (T). Loaned to SAOEU between 24 September 1996 and 17 March 1997 it then received an upgrade to Jaguar 96 standard by November 1998. Transferred to No. 6 Squadron as 'ED following overhaul in October 2005 it remained with the unit until disbandment. It was finally flown to RAF Cosford for instructional duties where it still resided in November 2013.

XX739

S36 F/F 17 September 1974 (E. Bucklow) and D/D to RAF Lossiemouth 23 October 1974 for No. 226 OCU code '12'. The aircraft was transferred to No. 6 Squadron on 31 July 1975 and repainted into wrap-around all-over camouflage scheme at No. 5 MU in August 1977. Noted carrying a white square on tail- and upper-wing surfaces in October 1980 and coded 'EE' in February 1981 it was assigned to the Gibraltar Detachment (Gib Det) as 'I'. It then went into store at RAF Shawbury in October 1985. It was later assigned to ground instructional duties in December 1986 at No. 1 SoTT RAF Halton with maintenance serial 8902M. It was then transferred first to RAF Cosford until at least April 2005 and then to RAF Syerston by April 2007 but was disposed of to Dick Everett on 1 May 2014. It was stored at the former RAF Bentwaters but was sold to the 'Delta Force' Paintball Park, Upminster, relocating on 10 June 2016.

XX740

S37 F/F 25 September 1974 (A.M. Love) and D/D to RAF Lossiemouth 23 October 1974 for No. 6 Squadron. The jet went to Coltishall on 6 November 1974 and, following overhaul with No. 60 MU and transfer to JMU, was identified as a candidate for loan to India. It was flown to Warton as G-27-331 on 17 March 1980. However, following upgrade to Jaguar International standard, it suffered a nose wheel collapse on

landing on 23 April 1980. It was later delivered to India on 14 August 1980 as JI 017. It was returned to Warton, UK on 19 April 1984 against future export orders and sold to Oman as 225, departing the UK on 4 November 1986.

XX741

S38 F/F 4 October 1974 (J. Preece) and D/D RAF Lossiemouth 18 November 1974 for No. 226 OCU code '13'. Following overhaul at No. 60 MU in November 1975 it was reissued to No. 54 Squadron eventually becoming 'GL' in February 1981. The jet was then transferred to No. 6 Squadron and upgraded to GR.1A with code 'EJ'. Receiving a desert-pink ARTF scheme in August 1990 it was then sent to the Gulf in the interim of stage three, the upgraded aircraft arriving in October 1990. It was returned to the UK before conflict, regaining its original scheme and code. The aircraft was transferred to No. 226 OCU as '04' by September 1993 and sent to RAF Shawbury for long-term store by August 1994. Still current in September 2005 it was put up for disposal by tender under DSAT 3146 on 26 May 2005. It departed Shawbury by road for D. Everett Aero, Sproughton on 18 November 2005. XX741 now resides in the Cold War Museum at the former RAF Bentwaters.

XX742

S39 F/F 21 October 1974 (E. Bucklow) and D/D to Boscombe Down 15 November 1974 for engine-stall trials behind a Victor K.2, and later to RAF Lossiemouth on 9 December 1974 for No. 226 OCU code '14'. Following overhaul at No. 60 MU between 30 October 1975 and 10 December 1975, reissued to No. 6 Squadron on 5 January 1976. It received white square markings on its tail and upper-wing surfaces in October 1980 and was coded 'EF'

in February 1981. The aircraft crashed into the North Sea 40 miles off Bacton, Norfolk on 19 April 1983 with the pilot ejecting safely.

XX743

S40 F/F 30 October 1974 (E. Bucklow) and D/D to RAF Coltishall 26 November 1974 for No. 6 Squadron. Coded 'EG' in February 1981 passed into store at RAF Shawbury on 5 February 1985 and assigned to ground instructional duties at RAF Halton as 8949M where it was noted in March 1988. It was reassigned to No. 2 SoTT at RAF Cosford on 29 September 1994 upon the closure of Halton and is still in use.

XX744

S41 F/F 7 November 1974 (E. Bucklow) and D/D Boscombe Down 5 December 1974 for use by A&AEE. Returned to Warton on 18 June 1975 and reissued to No. 17 Squadron by July 1976 it received the temporary code 'S'. Following overhaul at the JMU it transferred to No. 14 Squadron in May 1978 as 'BU' before changing to 'BG' by September 1978; to No. 6 Squadron, becoming 'EH' in February 1981 but back in Germany with No. 31 Squadron as 'DG' by June 1981. Moved to No. 17 Squadron as 'BA' in September 1983 and back to No. 31 Squadron as 'DJ' in January 1984. Flown to RAF Shawbury for storage on 7 February 1985, it was transferred to Warton by July 1993 as a possible resale contender to Ecuador but this never materialised. Returned to store at RAF Shawbury by August 1994 the aircraft then went to ground instructional duties at RAF Coltishall in May 1998. Sold to the Dick Everett collection at Sproughton, Suffolk by October 2002. XX744 was later disposed of to a paintball park at Abridge by November 2009 and still current in September 2015.

XX745

S42 F/F 5 November 1974 (E. Bucklow) and D/D to RAF Lossiemouth 16 December 1974 for No. 226 OCU code '15'. Following overhaul at No. 60 MU and then repainting into the wraparound all-over camouflage scheme at No. 5 MU in October 1976 the jet was reassigned to No. 20 Squadron as code 'CU'. It was then transferred to No. 6 Squadron on 9 March 1979 and coded 'EJ' in February 1981. At JMU in early 1984 it was upgraded to GR.1A and reissued to No. 54 Squadron as 'GN' in May 1984. It returned to No. 226 OCU on December 1986, taking up the code '03' before returning to No. 6 Squadron on 5 August 1988 as 'EB'. Once again it was then sent to No. 226 OCU on 7 March 1989, this time as '04', retaining that code when unit became No. 16 (Reserve) Squadron. It returned to No. 6 Squadron in August 1993 as 'EG' before receiving the new grey colour scheme at St Athan. It was once again assigned to No. 16 (Reserve) Squadron in November 1996 as a GR.1A before transfer to No. 54 Squadron as 'GV' by May 1999. It was involved in a collision with XX832 in July 2000 resulting in damage to the forward fuselage section. It travelled by road from RAF Leuchars to St Athan on 25 November 2000 and then to store at RAF Shawbury until February 2004 before going to Boscombe Down for instruction duties and to provide a spares source for XX833. The jet was eventually scrapped, with the nose section being acquired by No. 1350 Squadron/ATC (Air Training Corps) at Fareham by October 2009.

XX746

S43 F/F 4 December 1974 (E. Bucklow) and D/D to RAF Lossiemouth 20 December 1974 for No. 226 OCU as code '16'. Repainted in overall wraparound camouflage scheme at No. 5 MU in February 1977 it was then placed in short-term store with JMU at Abingdon. It was issued to No. 31 Squadron in late 1977 becoming code 'DE' but transferred to No. 6 Squadron on 2 April 1979, later becoming 'EK' in February 1981. It was moved to No. 17 Squadron on 19 August 1982 as 'BD' and then onto No. 14 Squadron by June 1984 as 'AB'. It returned to RAF Lossiemouth on 4 November 1985 to once again join No. 226 OCU, this time as code '09', although this was short lived as it was placed in store at RAF Shawbury shortly afterwards. Assigned to ground instructional duties and allocated maintenance serial 8895M it was delivered to No. 1 SoTT at RAF Halton by August 1986. Upon closure of this facility it relocated to RAF Cosford marked as code 'S' where it still resides.

XX747

S44 F/F 4 December 1974 (E. Bucklow) and D/D RAF Lossiemouth for No. 226 OCU code '17'. Repainted into an all-over wraparound camouflage at No. 5 MU in April 1976 it was reissued to No. 54 Squadron by February 1980 for that unit to take the aircraft to Red Flag. Transferred to No. 17 Squadron on 18 January 1983 becoming 'BA', by September 1983 it had moved onto No. 31 Squadron as 'DG' and finally No. 20 Squadron as 'CH' two months later. It went to No. 6 Squadron as 'EK' by August 1984 forming part of 'Gib Det' as 'B' before being retired to RAF Shawbury by October 1985. It was allocated to ground instructional duties with No. 1 SoTT RAF Halton and was given the maintenance serial 8903M and received ARTF desert-pink scheme with spurious 'Sadman' nose art (ala XZ364). Upon closure of that facility it was transferred to the Aircraft Maintenance Instruction Flight at RAF Cranwell for use by the Airframe Technology Flight where it, or at least part of it, resided until November 2003 when acquired by Dick Everett at Sproughton.

XX748

S45 F/F 24 December 1974 (E. Bucklow) and D/D to RAF Lossiemouth 5 February 1975 for No. 226 OCU as code '20'. Placed in short-term store with JMU by October 1977 it had returned to the unit again by August 1979. Reissued to No. 14 Squadron as 'AA' on 15 August 1983 but transferred to Coltishall in October 1985 for No. 54 Squadron where it took up the code 'GK'. Then in February 1987 it was given the code 'GD'. The jet went to RAF Shawbury for short-term store by February 1989 but to JMU for Gulf War upgrade in May 1990 and outshopped in desert-pink ARTF on 2 October 1990, with the aircraft departing for Thumrait on 2 November 1990. It returned on 12 March 1991 coded 'U' on NWD and sporting thirty-six mission symbols. Back in normal camouflage and as 'GK' by June 1991 it was dispatched to Boscombe Down as one of three aircraft to receive the stage three upgrade allowing the use of TIALD. The aircraft was initially designated GR.1B then, following attention at St Athan in July 2000, GR.3 and finally GR.3A. it was retained by the squadron as 'GK' until disbandment then passed to No. 6 Squadron and was allocated code 'EG' March 2005, remaining as such until March 2007 when the squadron disbanded. It was flown to RAF Cosford on 18 May 2007 for instructional duties where it still resides.

XX749

S46 F/F 14 February 1975 (E. Bucklow) and D/D RAF Lossiemouth 14 February 1975 for No. 226

OCU as code '21'. Suffered a nose wheel collapse whilst hangared on 18 April 1975 and did not fly again until 10 June 1976. It went to No. 5 MU for repainting into wraparound all-over camouflage on 23 June 1976 and then to No. 60 MU for overhaul on 20 July 1976. The aircraft crashed on return to the unit on 10 December 1979 after colliding with XX755 near Lumsden, West Aberdeenshire with the loss of the pilot.

XX750

S47 F/F 16 January 1975 (P. Millett) and D/D to RAF Lossiemouth 17 February 1975 for No. 226 OCU code '22'. It was repainted in the all-over wraparound camouflage at No. 5 MU in April 1976 followed by overhaul at the JMU. It returned to the unit but transferred to No. 14 Squadron as 'AL' on May 1983, only to crash in the Nellis Range area during Red Flag on 7 February 1984 with the loss of the No. 6 Squadron pilot.

XX751

S48 F/F 27 January 1975 (E. Bucklow) and D/D to RAF Coltishall 14 April 1975 for onward transfer two days later to No. 14 Squadron where it was coded 'X'. Transferred to No. 226 OCU on 10 December 1975 becoming code '10' and repainted into the wraparound all-over camouflage at No. 5 MU in April 1976. Placed in store at RAF Abingdon and relegated to ground instructional duties by March 1988 when assigned maintenance serial 8937M with No. 2 SoTT at RAF Cosford until at least April 2005 before transfer to RAF Syerston, where it remained until 29 April 2014 when it was moved to the former RAF Bentwaters.

XX752

S49 F/F 7 February 1975 (P. Ginger) and D/D to RAF Coltishall 4 March 1975 for use by No. 54 Squadron. Following overhaul at No. 60 MU it was transferred to No. 226 OCU as code '06' only to be sent to No. 5 MU for repainting into the all-over wraparound camouflage scheme. It was placed into short-term store with JMU in March 1980 and later upgraded to GR.1A before issue back to No. 54 Squadron as 'GF' in May 1984. Again placed into store, this time at RAF Shawbury, by December 1988 until 29 October 1990 when it was sent back to the JMU still marked as 54/GF. It was reissued to No. 6 Squadron as 'EQ' by June 1991. It was upgraded to GR.3A whilst at St Athan between 6 September 1999 and 22 February 2000 and issued to No. 16 (Reserve) Squadron as 'D' on 1 March 2000 then subsequently 'PD'. The aircraft went to No. 41 Squadron as 'FC' by December 2001 and painted in ARTF arctic colour scheme in November 2003 for Exercise Snow Goose at Bardufoss. It returned to normal grey on 8 December 2003 and was reassigned to No. 6 Squadron as 'EK' in March 2005 until disbandment. XX752's last flight was on 12 June 2007 where it flew to RAF Cosford for instructional duties.

XX753

S50 F/F 24 February 1975 (E. Bucklow) and D/D to RAF Coltishall 27 March 1975 for use by No. 6 Squadron. Following overhaul by No. 60 MU it was transferred to No. 226 OCU on 2 July 1976 taking up the code '05'. It was later repainted at No. 5 MU into the all-over wraparound camouflage scheme during August 1977 and loaned to No. 54 Squadron for Exercise Red Flag in February 1980. The aircraft went into store at RAF Shawbury by November 1990 and

with the maintenance serial 9087M the cockpit section was allocated to RAF Exhibition Flight at RAF Abingdon by July 2004. It was finally sold to Newark Air Museum on 23 April 2010 where it resides today.

XX754

S51 F/F 12 March 1975 (J. Cockburn) and D/D to RAF Lossiemouth 22 April 1975 for No. 226 OCU code '23'. The jet was repainted into all-over wraparound camouflage at No. 5 MU in June 1976 and later loaned to No. 54 Squadron for Exercise Red Flag 2-80. It was reassigned to No. 14 Squadron on 21 September 1984 as 'AL' then went back to No. 226 OCU in March 1985. After being upgraded to GR.1A at JMU in January 1987 it was transferred to No. 54 Squadron as 'GR', later going to No. 6 Squadron by June 1990 as 'EQ'. It went to JMU in September 1990 for Gulf War upgrades, emerging in a desert-pink ARTF finish. It was delivered to the unit at Thumrait on 2 November 1990 but crashed prior to hostilities on 13 November 1990 in Qatar 100 miles south of Bahrain with the loss of the pilot.

XX755

S52 F/F 12 March 1975 (E. Bucklow) and D/D to RAF Coltishall 14 April 1975 prior to delivery two days later to RAF Bruggen for use by No. 14 Squadron. Initially coded 'A' it was only on squadron strength until 7 October 1975 when it was transferred to No. 226 OCU as '08'. Repainted at No. 5 MU into the all-over wraparound camouflage during April 1976 it crashed on 10 December 1979 near to Lumsden, West Aberdeenshire after colliding with XX749.

XX756

S53 F/F 21 March 1975 (E. Bucklow) and D/D to RAF Bruggen 23 April 1975 for No. 14 Squadron as code 'B'. It was the first Jaguar delivered directly to Germany. It was reassigned to No. 226 OCU on 8 October 1975 as code '07' and was repainted into all-over wraparound camouflage at No. 5 MU in November 1976. Transferring to No. 20 Squadron as 'CB' in March 1984 it then moved to No. 14 Squadron as 'AB' in July 1984 before returning to RAF Coltishall in October 1985. It was assigned the maintenance serial 8899M and allocated to ground instructional duties at No. 2 SoTT RAF Cosford by August 1986 where it resides today with the code 'W'.

XX757

S54 F/F 3 April 1975 (A. Love) and D/D to RAF Bruggen 6 May 1975 for No. 14 Squadron code 'E'. Transferred to No. 226 OCU on 17 October 1975 taking the code '12' and was repainted into the all-over wraparound camouflage at No. 5 MU in March 1976. It was reassigned to No. 20 Squadron as 'CU' in early 1980 and placed into store at RAF Shawbury on 4 July 1984 where, by March 1988, it had been assigned to the ground instructional role. Allocated the maintenance serial 8948M with No. 1 SoTT at RAF Halton it subsequently moved to RAF Cosford with the closure of that station. Coded 'CU' it remained in instructional use until January 2012 when it was presented to the Brazilian Air Force Museum at Campo dos Afonsos.

XX758

S55 F/F 11 April 1975 (E. Bucklow) and D/D to RAF Bruggen for No. 14 Squadron as 'C'. Transferred to No. 226 OCU on 30 October 1975 becoming code '18' it was repainted with all-over wraparound camouflage at No. 5 MU in August 1977. Upon return to the unit it subsequently crashed 14 miles west of

Dingwall on 18 November 1981 with the loss of the pilot.

XX759

S56 F/F 18 April 1975 (E. Bucklow) and D/D RAF Bruggen 1 May 1975 for No. 14 Squadron code 'D'. It was reassigned to No. 226 OCU on 14 October 1975 becoming code '19'. It undertook repairs at No. 60 MU following a bird strike in June 1976 and repainted at No. 5 MU Kemble in January 1977. It was returned to the unit and was the first aircraft to receive the revised unit markings, only to be lost in an accident on 1 November 1978 near Selkirk.

XX760

S57 F/F 30 April 1975 (P. Millett) and D/D to RAF Bruggen 22 May 1975 for No. 14 Squadron as 'F'. Reassigned to No. 226 OCU 20 November 1976 taking code '26' and then to No. 5 MU for repainting as the first aircraft into all-over wraparound camouflage scheme during March 1976. It went to No. 60 MU for overhaul and was redelivered to No. 14 Squadron as 'AA' in December 1976. The aircraft later crashed on 13 September 1982 2 miles north of Braegrudie on the Dalreavoch Estate, Rogart, Sutherland. The pilot ejected safely.

XX761

S58 F/F 24 April 1975 (E. Bucklow) and D/D to RAF Bruggen on 4 June 1975 for No. 14 Squadron as 'G'. It went to No. 226 OCU on 18 November 1975 taking the code '11' but was destroyed in a ground fire at RAF Lossiemouth after an engine explosion on 6 June 1978. The remains are used for ground instruction and the nose section was later reported at Warton, assigned maintenance serial 8600M. It later went to Boscombe Down for preservation, remaining

there until the collection moved to Old Sarum where it is still current.

XX762

S59 F/F 14 May 1975 (E. Bucklow) and D/D to RAF Bruggen on 4 June 1975. Reassigned to No. 226 OCU on 30 March 1976 becoming code '28' with the unit. Repainted into all-over wraparound camouflage at No. 5 MU in May 1976 it was later lost in a crash on 23 November 1979 200ft up on Chleibh, near Dalmally, Argyllshire. The pilot was killed.

XX763

S60 F/F 12 May 1975 (E. Bucklow) and D/D to RAF Lossiemouth 26 June 1975 for No. 226 OCU code '24'. Repainted at No. 5 MU into all-over wraparound camouflage in March 1977 it was then loaned to No. 54 Squadron in January 1980. Placed into store at RAF Shawbury by April 1985 it was later assigned to ground instructional duties with No. 4 SoTT at St Athan, the DARA Technical School, with maintenance serial 9009M, remaining there until at least March 2006. Reported as going to Winterpick Business Park, Wineham, Sussex in July 2006 it now forms part of the Hurn Aviation Museum, arriving there on 26 September 2009.

XX764

S61 F/F 7 June 1975 (E. Bucklow) and D/D to RAF Bruggen 2 July 1975 for No. 14 Squadron as 'J'. It was reassigned to No. 226 OCU on 20 November 1975 taking the code '27' and repainted into the all-over wraparound camouflage at No. 5 MU during April 1976. It was loaned to No. 6 Squadron during November 1988 and was recoded within No. 226 OCU to '13' before passing into store at RAF Shawbury on 3 September 1984. The jet was allocated to ground instructional duties with No. 4 SoTT St Athan, the DARA Technical School, by July 1989 and assigned maintenance serial 9010M, remaining there until at least April 2005. It then went to Blackstone, Sussex in February 2007 before passing to a private collector at 'Terry's Farm', Woodmancote in July 2009 where it is still current.

XX765

S62 F/F 13 June 1975 (P. Ginger) and D/D to RAF Bruggen 2 July 1975 for No. 14 Squadron but loaned to No. 17 Squadron before reassignment to No. 226 OCU on 3 December 1975, becoming code '27' with that unit. Repainted into the all-over wraparound camouflage at No. 5 MU in June 1976 then placed in store with JMU. Bailed back to BAE Systems and flown to Warton on 4 August 1978 by Eric Bucklow to be fitted with the Dowty-Boulton Paul Fly-By-Wire system, with a long-term project of a carbon-fibre wing. F/F as FBW was on 20 October 1981 with Chris Yeo at the controls and the aircraft sporting Royal Aircraft Establishment (RAE) red, white and blue corporate colours. Its F/F in its Active Control Technology (ACT) form with enlarged leading edge extensions was on 15 March 1984. Project completed and aircraft placed in store at Warton by May 1987. By March 1990 it had been resprayed olive green and received the inscription 'ACT' in light blue on the fin. It was then stored again and transferred to RAF Cosford, although it was back at Warton on 15 September 1999. Currently preserved as part of the RAF Museum collection at RAF Cosford.

XX766

S63 F/F 14 June 1975 (P. Ginger) and D/D to RAF Bruggen 8 July 1975 for No. 17 Squadron. It was reassigned to No. 226 OCU on 18 December 1975 taking the code '14'. Loaned to No. 54

Squadron for Exercise Red Flag 2-80 and upgraded to GR.1A at the JMU in January 1984, it was then reissued to No. 54 Squadron as 'GP'. It was transferred to No. 6 Squadron as 'EC' post maintenance in February 1989 as a GR.1A and later to receive 75th anniversary markings. Recoded 'EA' by May 1990 and later receiving stage three modifications including overwing missile rails and Sky Guardian RWR. A new grey colour scheme was applied in September 1995. It went to St Athan for short-term store in January 1998 and upgraded to GR.3 before issue to No. 16 (Reserve) Squadron as 'PE' on 31 May 2001. Painted in special marks for the 2001 display season it later returned to St Athan for major overhaul on 10 September 2004 and was issued to No. 6 Squadron as 'EF' on 24 June 2005. The aircraft returned to St Athan on 19 October 2005 and then moved to RAF Cosford for instructional duties on 31 January 2006 with where it is still current.

XX767

S64 F/F 25 June 1975 (E. Bucklow) and D/D to RAF Bruggen 18 May 1975 for No. 14 Squadron. It was reassigned to No. 226 OCU on 29 October 1975 becoming code '25' and repainted at No. 5 MU into all-over wraparound camouflage during March 1977. Placed into short-term store at the JMU on 21 April 1977 it was then returned to No. 14 Squadron as 'AU' but changing to 'AN' by July 1979. It was later transferred to No. 31 Squadron as 'DC' by September 1983, to No. 17 Squadron 'BD' by October 1984 and back with No. 226 OCU as '17' by March 1985. The jet was upgraded to GR.1A at JMU and issued to No. 54 Squadron on 26 September 1986 becoming code 'GE'. It had an ARTF arctic camouflage applied for Exercise Strong Resolve in February 1995 and then received stage three modifications variously quoted as

GR.1B or GR.1A (T). It received a new grey colour scheme in August 1996 and upgraded to GR.3A at St Athan between March 2000 and July 2000. The aircraft served with No. 54 Squadron until disbandment and was then reassigned to No. 41 Squadron as 'FK' in March 2005. It went to RAF Shawbury for store in April 2006 until transfer to RAF Cosford on 20 March 2007 for instructional duties.

XX768

S65 F/F 2 July 1975 (E. Bucklow) and D/D to RAF Bruggen 12 August 1975 for No. 14 Squadron but transferred to No. 17 Squadron by January 1976 becoming code 'BA'. It then went to No. 5 MU for painting into all-over wraparound camouflage in January 1977 but crashed near Heinsberg-Randerath on 29 September 1982 following a rear-end fire.

XX817

S66 F/F 10 July 1975 (J. Cockburn) and D/D to RAF Bruggen 20 August 1975 for No. 17 Squadron. It was coded 'BB' by June 1976 and received an all-over wraparound camouflage scheme at No. 5 MU in March 1977. The aircraft was lost on 17 July 1980 when it crashed in woods 7 miles from Bruggen with the pilot ejecting successfully.

XX818

S67 F/F 10 July 1975 (D. Eagles) and D/D to RAF Bruggen 15 August 1975 for No. 17 Squadron. It was coded 'BC' by May 1976 and later transferred to No. 20 Squadron as 'CC' by March 1977 and then to No. 31 Squadron as 'DE' by November 1983. It returned to the UK on 2 November 1984 for storage at RAF Shawbury and assigned to ground instructional duties with maintenance serial 8945M. Initially it was sent to No. 1 SoTT at RAF Halton in March 1988 but following the former's closure it moved to RAF Cosford where it still resides today.

XX819

S68 F/F 5 August 1975 (P. Ginger) and D/D to RAF Bruggen 20 August 1975 for No. 17 Squadron. Assigned code 'BD' it was transferred to No. 20 Squadron by November 1978 to become 'CE'. Loaned to No. 226 OCU in February 1982 it was dispatched for storage at RAF Shawbury on 25 May 1984 and assigned to ground instructional duties. Allocated maintenance serial 8923M it was sent to No. 2 SoTT RAF Cosford by January 2000 where it still remains to this day.

XX820

S69 F/F 13 August 1975 (E. Bucklow) and D/D to RAF Bruggen 3 September 1975 for No. 17 Squadron. Coded 'BE' by June 1976 it was transferred to No. 20 Squadron as 'CE' by June 1977 and back to No. 17 Squadron again by November 1978 as 'BD'. The aircraft crashed on 11 June 1982 whilst being operated by No. 31 Squadron, when on final approach to RAF Bruggen, with the pilot ejecting safely.

XX821

S70 F/F 14 August 1975 (A. Love) and D/D to RAF Bruggen 1 September 1975 for No. 17 Squadron. Coded 'BF' by June 1976 it was transferred to No. 14 Squadron by September 1983 becoming code 'AN' then reassigned to No. 41 Squadron as 'P' in March 1985. The jet passed into storage and was then assigned to ground instructional role with maintenance serial 8896M in the Servicing Instructional Flight (SIF) at RAF Cranwell on 30 July 1986. It was finally transferred to RAF Cosford with the flight where it is still current.

XX822

S71 F/F 29 August 1975 (P. Millett) and D/D to RAF Bruggen 22 September 1975 for No. 14 Squadron where it was assigned the code 'AA'. The aircraft crashed 15 miles north of Ahlhorn on 2 July 1976.

XX823

S72 F/F 22 August 1975 (A. Love) and D/D to RAF Bruggen 15 September 1975 for No. 17 Squadron with code 'BG'. Aircraft crashed into a hill on 25 July 1978 near Cagliari, Sardinia whilst the unit was on APC at Decimomannu.

XX824

S73 F/F 2 September 1975 (A. Love) and D/D to RAF Bruggen 23 September 1975 for No. 14 Squadron as 'A'. It was recoded 'AB' before being transferred to No. 17 Squadron by September 1978 as 'BH'. It was reassigned to No. 14 Squadron following overhaul at the JMU in late 1984 becoming code 'AD', but was retired to RAF Shawbury in November 1985 and assigned to ground instructional duties at RAF Halton by January 1990 with maintenance serial 9019M. It was relocated to RAF Cosford when Halton closed the jet and is still current in the instructional role.

XX825

S74 F/F 14 September 1975 (R. Stock) and D/D to RAF Bruggen 16 October 1975 for No. 14 Squadron where it became code 'AC'. It was transferred to No. 31 Squadron as 'DA' by October 1983 and No. 17 Squadron as 'BN' by October 1984; it was then flown back to RAF Shawbury for storage. Allocated to the ground instructional role and assigned the maintenance serial 9020M it was first used at No. 1 SoTT RAF Halton, then with No. 2 SoTT at RAF Cosford where it resides today.

XX826

S75 F/F 12 September 1975 (D. Eagles) and D/D to RAF Bruggen 16 October 1975 for No. 14 Squadron. Initially coded 'B' this was altered to 'AD' by June 1976. It received all-over wraparound camouflage at No. 5 MU in November 1976 and was reassigned to No. 20 Squadron as 'CA' by October 1983 before passing to No. 2 (Army Co-operation (AC)) Squadron in July 1984 taking up the code '34'. Flown to RAF Shawbury for storage on 5 March 1985 and relegated to ground instructional use at RAF Cosford by March 1990. Assigned the maintenance serial 9021M at Cosford it was up for disposal by tender through DSAT 3147 of June 2005. The jet went to Dick Everett at Sproughton and was noted there in September 2006 and March 2007. It then went to Hinstock in February 2012 and finally the Shannon Museum by April 2014.

XX827

S76 F/F 22 September 1975 (A. Love) and D/D to RAF Bruggen 6 October 1975 for No. 14 Squadron as code 'C'. Recoded 'AE' by June 1976 and repainted into all-over wraparound camouflage at No. 5 MU in December 1976; the aircraft was then reassigned to No. 20 Squadron as 'CL' on 8 March 1977. Transferred to No. 17 Squadron as 'BM' by September 1978 it was lost in a crash over the Nellis Range on 12 February 1981.

XX828

B16 F/F 7 October 1974 (A. Love/P. Ginger) and used in Forces Aérea Venezuela (FAV) evaluation. D/D to RAF Lossiemouth 7 November 1974 for No. 226 OCU as code 'P'. It crashed on 1 June 1981, 5 miles north of Forfar with both crew ejected safely.

Not blessed with excessive power the Jaguar could still be an impressive performer. XX832, seen here with No. 16 Squadron in the vertical climb, it now resides with one of the museums at Chino, California.

XX829

B17 F/F 28 November 1974 (D. Eagles/R. Taylor) and D/D to RAF Coltishall 23 December 1974 for No. 54 Squadron. Coded 'GT' in February 1981 it was transferred to No. 6 Squadron as 'ER' by January 1985 and then upgraded to T.2A. Loaned to No. 226 OCU in February 1986 it was back with No. 6 Squadron as 'ET' on 10 January 1989, by which time it was sporting the legend 'Flying Canopeners' in red beneath the RWR. Reassigned to No. 16 (Reserve) Squadron as 'Y' by March 1994 it was then moved to No. 54 Squadron as 'GZ' in May 1994. The jet finally passed into store at RAF Shawbury on 6 March 2001, although was up for disposal by tender DSAT 3146 of 26 May 2005. Destined for Everett Aero, Sproughton it was last noted there in August 2007 before being sold to Newark Air Museum by March 2012.

XX830

B18 F/F 25 November 1974 (E. Bucklow/R. Kenward) and D/D to RAF Lossiemouth 20 December 1974 for No. 226 OCU as code 'R'. Loaned to A&AEE in April 1985 then, following overhaul at the JMU in November 1986, was transferred permanently to the ETPS. Placed in store at St Athan in November 1996 then Shawbury in February 1999. The fuselage was taken by road to Warton on 29 September 1999 for T.2A upgrade development. Following this it was removed once again by road to RAF Coltishall on 6 July 2000 where the cockpit was preserved and the fuselage was moved onward to Bruntingthorpe for component reclamation and then scrapped. It has an alloy maintenance serial 9293M. As part of the Mick Jennings collection it passed to the City of Norwich Aviation Museum when RAF Coltishall closed and is still current.

XX831

B19 F/F 10 December 1974 (A. Love/V. Malings) and used on flights six through twenty-three on flame out investigations. D/D to RAF Lossiemouth 21 March 1975 for No. 226 OCU code 'W' but crashed shortly afterwards on 30 April 1975.

XX832

B20 F/F 16 December 1974 (A. Love/V. Malings) and D/D to RAF Lossiemouth 3 February 1975 for No. 226 OCU as code 'S'. It remained with the unit until placed in short-term store at RAF Shawbury in January 1991. Following overhaul at St Athan on 12 May 1995 the aircraft, now sporting the new grey colour scheme, was assigned to No. 16 (Reserve) Squadron code 'Z'. Transferred to No. 6 Squadron as 'EZ' by September 1999, reportedly as a T.2A, it suffered an in-flight collision with XX745 that necessitated another visit to St Athan on 13 July 2000. Returning to Coltishall on 16 February 2001 it was flown to RAF Shawbury for storage on 12 October 2001 where it resides today, although up for disposal by tender through DSAT 3146 on 26 May 2005. Destined for Everett Aero, Sproughton but put on display at former USAFE base at Bentwaters until May 2013, it was then sold to one of the Chino museums in California.

XX833

B21 F/F 17 January 1975 (E. Bucklow/R. Kenward) and D/D to RAF Lossiemouth 21 February 1975 for No. 226 OCU code 'T'. It was transferred to No. 20 Squadron as 'CZ' by early 1977 before passing onto No. 14 Squadron as 'AZ' in April 1984. Upgraded to T.2A and reissued to No. 41 Squadron as 'Z' by June 1986 it

XX833.

was initially loaned, and then permanently assigned to 'A' Flight RAE Farnborough. Noted wearing the code N2 in May 1989 and the CTTO badge in January 1990, it had by then been transferred to the DRA Experimental Flying Squadron at Boscombe Down as the TIALD research aircraft. Named *Night Cat* and redesignated T.2B (or possibly T.2A (T)) it has remained with QinetiQ. During overhaul at St Athan in September 1996 it received the new grey colour scheme, remaining on strength until 20 December 2007 when it undertook the final RAF Jaguar flight and was delivered to RAF Cosford for instructional duties.

XX834

B22 F/F 5 February 1975 (A. Love/R. Stock) and D/D RAF Lossiemouth 17 March 1975 for No. 226 OCU code 'U'. It was transferred to No. 14 Squadron as 'AY' by October 1978 although was back with No. 226 OCU shortly afterwards. By August 1984 it had been reissued to No. 2 (AC) Squadron as '37' then recoded '34' by May 1985, finally transferring to No. 6 Squadron as 'EZ' where it was lost in a crash on 7 August 1988 when it struck high-tension wires near Wildbad-Kreuth, West Germany with the loss of the pilot, although the USAF back seater ejected safely.

XX835

B23 F/F 14 February 1975 (E. Bucklow/J. Evans) and D/D to RAF Lossiemouth 17 March 1975 for No. 226 OCU code 'V'. Loaned to RAE in September 1986 and upgraded to T.2B, it was reissued to No. 54 Squadron on 10 October

Starting to taxi from RAF Coltishall for the last time XX835 is being flown by Air Commodore Graham Wright as he prepares to lead the Coltishall Finale in April 2006.

1995 with spells on No. 6 Squadron and No. 41 Squadron as 'FY'; it was flown to St Athan on 23 August 1999 for upgrade to T.4 returning to No. 41 Squadron afterwards. It was then assigned to No. 6 Squadron as 'EX' where it remained until disbandment. It was flown to RAF Cosford on 2 July 2007 for instructional duties.

XX836

B24 F/F 8 March 1975 (J. Cockburn/R. Woollett) and D/D 27 March 1975 to RAF Coltishall for No. 54 Squadron but was destined for No. 14 Squadron where it was redelivered on 7 April 1975. Coded 'AZ' it was transferred to No. 17 Squadron as 'BZ' on 28 August 1980. Following upgrade to T.2A at the JMU on 18 October 1985 it was reissued to No. 6 Squadron as 'ER'. The jet served with the unit until at least 1989

when it was relocated to RAF Shawbury for long-term store. It remained at Shawbury from at least August 1989 until 10 August 2005 when it was sold to Dick Everett, Sproughton, Suffolk following sale by tender DSAT 3146 of 26 May 2005. It was still current in April 2014.

XX837

B25 F/F 21 March 1975 (T. Ferguson/R. Stock) and D/D to RAF Lossiemouth 23 May 1975 for No. 226 OCU as code 'Z'. Placed in store at RAF Shawbury by July 1986 and then identified for ground instructional duties at No. 1 SoTT at RAF Halton where it arrived by June 1989. Assigned maintenance serial 8978M it relocated to RAF Cosford following the closure of Halton where it resides today coded initially 'I' and now 'Z'.

XX838

B26 F/F 5 April 1975 (E. Bucklow/R. Stock) and D/D to RAF Lossiemouth 29 April 1975 for No. 226 OCU code 'X'. Loaned to No. 17 Squadron on 1 December 1975 until 16 January 1976 it then went to No. 60 MU for overhaul before returning to No. 226 OCU. It was delivered to Warton on 16 May 1978 for evaluation by FAV including Brigadier General Bracho. The aircraft returned to Lossiemouth on 19 May 1978. Placed in short-term store at RAF Shawbury from September 1991 until 30 June 1998 it was then dispatched to St Athan for T.4 upgrade, and then on 5 May 1999 it was reissued to No. 16 (Reserve) Squadron as 'R' and on, moving to RAF Coltishall, recoded as 'PR'. At the demise of the unit it was assigned to No. 41 Squadron in March 2005 as 'FZ' and noted sporting a Union Jack and motif 'Jaguar Display 2005' on fin, but this was short-lived. The jet went to St Athan by March 2006 where it was WFU before being moved to the former RAF Bentwaters where it still resided in July 2013.

XX839

B27 F/F 18 April 1975 (T. Ferguson/R. Woollett) and D/D to RAF Lossiemouth 22 May 1975 for No. 226 OCU as 'Y'. The aircraft went to RAF Shawbury for a short period in store between July 1986 and May 1988 then, following overhaul at the JMU, returned to its original unit. Assigned to No. 54 Squadron as 'GW' by April 1995 it was discovered whilst on major overhaul to have structural problems and was retired to ground instructional duties post-October 1995. Assigned maintenance serial 9256M it was used by the DARA Civilian Technical Training School (CTTS) at St Athan until May 2002 when it was sold as scrap to Conifer Metals, Clay Cross, Chesterfield.

Retired from front-line service in the mid 1980s XX837 spent more than half of its career as an instructional airframe. Initially at RAF Halton, then RAF Cosford before being assigned to the Aircraft Maintenance Instruction Flight at RAF Cranwell where it became one of the few Jaguars to receive the RAF training all-black colour scheme. The jet later returned to Cosford when the flight relocated.

XX840

B28 F/F 17 May 1975 (E. Bucklow/R. Stock) and D/D to RAF Bruggen on 12 June 1975 for No. 17 Squadron as code 'BZ'. It was reassigned to No. 226 OCU as 'A' by September 1980 and, following T.2A upgrade at the JMU, was issued in February 1988 to No. 2 (AC) Squadron as '34' then code '33' and finally on demise of that unit to No. 41 Squadron as 'X' on 27 January 1989. Placed in short-term store at RAF Shawbury in October 1990 it remained there until transfer to St Athan on 24 September 1998 for T.4 upgrade. It was not immediately reissued to service but assigned to No. 16 (Reserve) Squadron in May 1999 as 'S', then recoded 'PS', until allocated to No. 6 Squadron as 'EY' following the former's disbandment. Remained with No. 6 Squadron until its last flight on 12 June 2007 to RAF Cosford for instructional duties.

XX840 was one of the last RAF Jaguars in service. It is seen here taxiing at RAF Coningsby during the final days of the squadron.

Sent for short-term store at RAF Shawbury in August 1994 it was reissued to No. 41 Squadron as 'FV' on 8 July 1996 following repainting into the new grey scheme. It was reassigned to No. 16 (Reserve) Squadron as 'X' then upgraded to T.4 at St Athan in October 2000. It was loaned to Warton as part of the Rolls-Royce Adour engine upgrade programme, returning to Coltishall 31 October 2002. Initially the aircraft went to No. 16 (Reserve) Squadron then on its disbandment to No. 41 Squadron as 'FX'. Following the disbandment of No. 41 Squadron the aircraft was flown to St Athan where it was WFU before passing to the former RAF Bentwaters by August 2006, and was last noted there in July 2013.

XX843

B31 F/F 24 June 1975 (T. Ferguson/R. Taylor) and D/D to RAF Lossiemouth 18 July 1975 for No. 226 OCU code 'W'. Reissued to No. 2 (AC) Squadron as 'T' by May 1976 it was subsequently recoded '33' then '36' before returning to JMU on 3 January 1985 for T.2A upgrade. Loaned to No. 226 OCU as 'E' in February 1986 it was reassigned to No. 54 Squadron as 'GT' in August 1987 but crashed on 29 August 1991 following a mid-air collision with a Cessna 152 over Carno, near Newtown, Powys. The two crew ejected but the rear-seater, a RAF Wing Commander (who had just returned to limited flying following a lung and heart transplant), was killed, as was the pilot of the Cessna.

XX844

B32 F/F 5 August 1975 (R. Stock/R. Woollett) and D/D to RAF Bruggen 27 August 1975 for use by No. 31 Squadron code 'DZ'. It was transferred to No. 17 Squadron as 'BY' by December 1983 then to No. 226 OCU as 'F' by April 1985. It was

XX841

B29 F/F 16 May 1975 (P. Ginger/V. Malings) and displayed at Paris Salon on 30 May 1975 returning to Warton 9 June 1975. D/D to RAF Lossiemouth 27 June 1975 for No. 226 OCU with the code 'K'. Reassigned to No. 41 Squadron as 'S' by April 1985, it then spent a short period in store at RAF Shawbury from May 1986 to early 1990 following which it was loaned to the ETPS. Transferring to No. 6 Squadron as 'ES' by June 1992 it was then upgraded at St Athan to T.4 in October 1999 emerging in the new grey colour scheme. The jet went to No. 16 (Reserve) Squadron as 'PQ' by February 2002 until disbandment when allocated to No. 6 Squadron as 'EW' where it remained until at least April 2006. WFU at RAF

Shawbury by February 2007 it was sold to Dick Everett by July 2007, who in turn sold it to a private collector in Royal Tunbridge Wells by June 2010.

XX842

B30 F/F 4 June 1975 (E. Bucklow/J. Evans) and D/D to RAF Lossiemouth 30 June 1975 for No. 226 OCU as code 'W'. It went to No. 54 Squadron on 31 July 1975 and then No. 41 Squadron as 'T' by September 1976. It was then transferred to No. 2 (AC) Squadron following overhaul at the JMU in late 1986 as '33'. Back to Coltishall, this time with No. 6 Squadron as 'EW', in October 1988 it then spent a period on loan to both the ETPS and RAE at Farnborough between 23 February 1989 and 12 June 1990.

then loaned to the A&AEE at Boscombe Down in July 1987 followed by a period with the Cranfield CIT in January 1990. The aircraft was then identified for ground instructional training and allocated the maintenance serial 9023M for use by No. 2 SoTT at RAF Cosford where it arrived in March 1990, but by January 1998 had been returned to St Athan for spares recovery, although still extant in September 1999.

XX845

B33 F/F 12 August 1975 (J. Cockburn/Krautlann (MBB pilot)) and D/D to RAF Bruggen 27 August 1975 for No. 17 Squadron code 'BY'. In March 1977 it went to No. 20 Squadron 'CZ' and then No. 2 (AC) Squadron in July 1977 where it was damaged on landing on 16 November 1977. It was taken to No. 431 MU for repairs and returned to flying status on 9 April 1979 returning to No. 2 (AC) Squadron as '34'. Following periods of use with No. 17 Squadron as 'BY' and No. 14 Squadron as 'AZ', as well as No. 226 OCU, it was reassigned to No. 41 Squadron as 'V' on 7 February 1989. Transferred to No. 226 OCU as 'A' in September 1993 it returned to Coltishall for No. 6 Squadron in June 1994 becoming 'ET'. It was upgraded to T.4 at St Athan in the March 2005 reshuffle and was assigned the code 'EV', but was flown to St Athan on 1 June 2005 for spares recovery. The aircraft went to DCAE Cosford by October 2005 but was declared surplus and moved to the fire and rescue training school at RNAS Predannock on 14 October 2009 where it still survives.

XX846

B34 F/F on 21 August 1975 (J. Cockburn/R. Kenward) but held by company to undertake Middle East sales tour between 13 November and 13 December 1975. It undertook its F/F

Jaguar T.4 of No. 6 Sqaudron venting fuel as it negotiates the Welsh valleys on a general handling sortie.

fitted with dash-26 engines on 4 November 1975. It then returned to Warton to undertake a series of demonstration flights with IAF pilot AVM Zaheer. With normal engines refitted it was test-flown on 28 January 1976 then D/D to RAF Lossiemouth 14 March 1976 for No. 226 OCU as 'A'. Reassigned to No. 14 Squadron as 'AZ' for a short period before returning to its former position with the OCU. The aircraft incurred a nose wheel collapse on landing at RAF Lossiemouth on 29 November 1984 but it had returned to flying by January 1985 and then upgraded to T.2A in September 1987. Loaned to the RAE on 23 November 1987 before reassignment as No. 41 Squadron 'Y' in August 1988. Another period of loan with ETPS took place in early February 1989 followed by a short period of store at RAF Shawbury from

27 February 1989 until September 1990 when it was overhauled at the JMU. Once again assigned to No. 226 OCU as 'A' in May 1992 it was issued to No. 41 Squadron as 'FY' by July 1993, then No. 16 (Reserve) Squadron as 'V' in February 1995 before recoding to 'PV' in June 2001. It was WFU by August 2004 and broken up for spares by 24 August 2005. The nose was noted at Coltishall in April 2006.

XX847

B35 F/F 23 October 1975 (E. Bucklow/J. Evans) and D/D to RAF Lossiemouth 10 November 1975 for No. 226 OCU code 'Q'. The jet went to No. 2 (AC) Squadron by June 1976 and then No. 14 Squadron as 'AY' in July 1986. It was sent for overhaul at JMU on 19 January 1980 becoming the 100th Jaguar to undergo overhaul with the unit. Returned to No. 14 Squadron on 1 July 1980 it was transferred to No. 20 Squadron as 'CZ' by April 1984 and then to No. 31 Squadron as 'DY' on 20 July 1984. Returned to UK in October 1984 and had been reissued to No. 226 OCU as 'G' by March 1985. Placed in short-term store at RAF Shawbury by July 1986, it remained there until returning to the JMU for upgrade in May 1990. To No. 41 Squadron as 'X' by April 1991 then 'FX' in March 1995 it was dispatched to St Athan by road for storage on 8 December 1995. The jet participated in the Jaguar fatigue test programme then upgraded to T.4 including the fitting of an upgraded Adour 106 engine. F/F in this configuration occurred on 26 June 2002. It was delivered to No. 16 (Reserve) Squadron in October 2002 as 'PY' before being allocated to No. 6 Squadron as 'EZ' in March 2005 where it remained until undertaking its last flight on 18 May 2007 to RAF Cosford for instructional duties.

XX915

B36 F/F 22 June 1976 (A. Love/R. Stock) and used for evaluation by Nigerian AF and D/D 20 July 1976 to ETPS at Boscombe Down. The jet was borrowed for the 1976 Society of British Aerospace Companies (SBAC) show where Canadian and Turkish AF pilots flew it. It was returned to Boscombe Down on 14 October 1976 but was borrowed again on 10 March 1978 for further IAF evaluation. The aircraft was lost in a crash on 17 January 1984 near to Porton Down, Wiltshire with the pilot ejecting safely.

XX916

B37 F/F 2 December 1976 (A. Love/R. Kenward) and D/D 18 January 1977 to ETPS at Boscombe Down. It was lost in a crash on 17 July 1981 in Bristol Channel off Hartland Point. Both crew ejected but one was killed.

XX955

S77 F/F 18 September 1975 (A. Love) and D/D to RAF Bruggen 6 October 1975 for No. 14 Squadron coded 'AF' by March 1976. It was repainted in wraparound camouflage at No. 5 MU in March 1977 and reissued to No. 17 Squadron as 'BC' by October 1983. Back with No. 14 Squadron as 'AN' by October 1984 it was then transferred to No. 54 Squadron in October 1985 becoming code 'GM'. It was upgraded to GR.1A at JMU in November 1986 and returned to No. 54 Squadron as 'GK'. Sent for storage at RAF Shawbury by October 1998; it remained there until sold by tender, DSAT 3146 of 26 May 2005, to the museum at Hermeskiel, Germany. The airframe departed Shawbury on 6 September 2005 for Dick Everett Aero at Sproughton, Suffolk but had arrived at the German museum by early October where it still resides currently.

XX956

S78 F/F 26 September 1975 (A. Love) and D/D to RAF Bruggen 22 October 1975 for No. 17 Squadron receiving code 'BH' by March 1976. Repainted into all-over wraparound camouflage at No. 5 MU in November 1976, it was transferred briefly to No. 14 Squadron as 'AB' in October 1978 but back with No. 17 Squadron by March 1979. It then transferred to No. 31 Squadron as 'DK' by August 1984 but was back with No. 17 Squadron as 'BE' by October 1984. Delivered to RAF Shawbury on 28 February 1985 for store it was identified for ground instructional training. The jet was allocated maintenance serial 8950M for use by No. 1 SoTT at RAF Halton where it had arrived by March 1988. It was transferred to RAF Cosford upon closure of Halton where it remained in use until 20 January 2009 when it was then moved to RAF Gibralter for gate-guard duties.

XX957

S79 F/F 3 October 1975 (R. Stock) and D/D to RAF Bruggen 24 October 1975 for No. 14 Squadron, taking up the code 'AG' by June 1976. It was transferred to No. 20 Squadron as 'CG' by March 1977 but crashed on approach to Bruggen on 21 October 1981 after being struck by lightning.

XX958

S80 F/F 7 October 1975 (E. Bucklow) and D/D to RAF Bruggen 24 October 1975 for use by No. 14 Squadron. It was coded 'AH' by May 1976. Noted sporting an ARTF arctic colour scheme in January 1980 it was transferred to No. 17 Squadron as 'BK' by December 1983. It was flown to RAF Shawbury on 12 March 1985 for storage and allocated to ground instructional duties as 9022M with No. 2 SoTT at RAF Cosford, arriving by March 1990 where it remains to this day.

XX959

S81 F/F 14 October 1975 (A. Love) and D/D to RAF Bruggen 4 November 1975 for No. 14 Squadron, adopting code 'AJ' by June 1976. It was transferred to No. 20 Squadron as 'CJ' by June 1977 and flown to RAF Shawbury for storage on 4 July 1984. Allocated to ground instructional duties at No. 2 SoTT RAF Cosford with maintenance serial 8959M, arriving by March 1988 where it still resides today.

XX960

S82 F/F 18 October 1975 (E. Bucklow) and D/D to RAF Bruggen 3 November 1975 for No. 14

Squadron receiving code 'AK' by March 1976. The aircraft crashed on 18 July 1979 near Iserlohn, West Germany with the pilot ejecting safely.

XX961

S83 F/F 20 October 1975 (A. Love) and D/D to RAF Bruggen 10 November 1975 for No. 17 Squadron where it had taken the code 'BJ' by June 1976. It was lost in a crash on 28 June 1980 following a collision with XX964 near Bruggen.

XX962

S84 F/F 30 October 1975 (E. Bucklow) and D/D to RAF Bruggen 13 November 1975 for No. 17 Squadron receiving code 'BK' by June 1976. Transferred to No. 20 Squadron as 'CK' by May 1977 it was back with No. 17 Squadron as 'BU' in November 1978. The jet was given the code 'BG' in November 1983 before relocating to Coltishall and No. 6 Squadron as 'EK' by August 1986. It was upgraded for Gulf operations and repainted in desert-pink ARTF before deploying to Thumrait on 2 November 1990 where it was coded 'X' and received the 'Fat Slags' nose art and thirty-seven mission symbols. It returned to the UK on 13 March 1991 and repainted into normal scheme by June 1991 as 'EK'. Sent to Boscombe Down it was one of the first three aircraft to receive TIALD modifications in February 1995, which together with the stage three modifications previously received saw its designation change to GR.1B. It participated in Operation Deliberate Force in 1995 sporting the grey (baby blue) ARTF scheme and where it had five mission symbols applied. It then lost its temporary colours by December 1995 and six months later was placed in store at Coltishall pending disposal. Dispatched to the Aircraft Maintenance

Another Aircraft Maintenance Training Flight Jaguar seen at RAF Cranwell. XX965 retains its former No. 16 Squadron markings.

Instruction Flight at RAF Cranwell and then by July 2002 to No. 1 SoTT at RAF Cosford coded 'P' and wearing the maintenance serial 9257M. It was declared surplus by February 2009 and was transferred to the Pembrey Ranges where it was still extant in July 2012.

XX963

S85 F/F 18 November 1975 (J. Cockburn) and D/D to RAF Bruggen 2 December 1975 for No. 14 Squadron receiving the code 'AL' by March 1976. The aircraft was lost in a crash on 25 May 1982 near Wesel, West Germany after an internal explosion caused by a strike by an AIM-9 sidewinder missile fired accidently by No. 92 Squadron Phantom FGR.2 XV422 'O'. Pilot ejected safely.

XX964

S86 F/F 11 November 1975 (D. Eagles) and D/D to RAF Bruggen 27 November 1975 for No. 17 Squadron receiving the code 'BL' by June 1976. It was lost following the collision with XX961 on 28 May 1980.

XX965

S87 F/F 6 November 1975 (E. Bucklow) and D/D to RAF Bruggen 21 November 1975 for No. 14 Squadron receiving code 'AM' by June 1976. It was upgraded to GR.1A at JMU in 1983 and reissued to No. 54 Squadron as 'GB' in August 1984. The jet went to No. 226 OCU as '04' on 6 March 1986 changing code to '07' in 1992 when it was used as the 1993 Jaguar display aircraft. On No. 226 OCU becoming No. 16

(Reserve) Squadron in March 1994 it took the code 'C' and was then placed into store at RAF Coltishall during January 1986. It passed to the Aircraft Maintenance Instruction Flight at RAF Cranwell as 9254M, remaining there until at least February 2010 where, shortly after the flight, it relocated to RAF Cosford taking with it the Jaguar airframes.

XX966

S88 F/F 19 November 1975 (D. Eagles) and D/D to RAF Bruggen 2 December 1975 for No. 17 Squadron, coded 'BM' by June 1976. It went to No. 20 Squadron as 'CL' by September 1978 then a short period of loan to A&AEE before returning to No. 20 Squadron on 27 October 1980 as 'CD'. It was upgraded to GR.1A followed with reissue to No. 54 Squadron as 'GK' in August 1984 and passing onto No. 6 Squadron as 'EL' by April 1985. It went to store at RAF Shawbury on 18 September 1985 and assigned to ground instructional training at No. 1 SoTT as 8904M by December 1986. Following the closure of RAF Halton the airframe was relocated to RAF Cosford after it was first displayed at Earls Court in August 1998. The aircraft arrived at Cosford shortly afterwards, coded 'J', where it remained until at least March 2009. It was declared surplus and moved to the Pembrey Ranges by October 2009 and was last noted in July 2012.

XX967

S89 F/F 24 November 1975 (A. Love) and undertook trials to prove modification on brake chute handle. D/D to RAF Bruggen 15 January 1976 for No. 31 Squadron where it was coded 'DA' by May 1976. It was transferred to No. 14 Squadron as 'AC' by October 1983 and then flown to storage at RAF Shawbury by November 1987. The aircraft was assigned to

ground instructional training at RAF Cosford as 9006M where it arrived in July 1989. It is still in use at Cosford today.

XX968

S90 F/F 24 November 1975 (E. Bucklow) and D/D to RAF Bruggen for No. 31 Squadron becoming 'DB' by June 1976. Transferred to No. 14 Squadron as 'AJ' by December 1983. It was retired to RAF Shawbury in November 1987 and allocated to the ground instructional role at RAF Cosford. Assigned the maintenance serial 9007M, it had arrived at Cosford by July 1989 where it still resides today.

XX969

S91 F/F 1 December 1975 (A. Love) and D/D to RAF Bruggen on 6 January 1976 for No. 31 Squadron receiving code 'DC' by June 1976. Transferred to No. 226 OCU on 14 November 1983 taking up the code '01' it was retired to RAF Cosford by August 1996, in the ground instructional role as 8897M, where it is still current today.

XX970

S92 F/F 8 December 1975 (J. Lee) and D/D to RAF Bruggen 6 January 1976 for No. 31 Squadron where by June 1976 it had taken up the code 'DD'. The aircraft suffered a landing mishap in 1982 and was passed to No. 431 MU for repairs. It was reissued to No. 17 Squadron as 'BJ' by October 1984 then to No. 226 OCU as '11' by April 1985 before moving to No. 6 Squadron on 28 January 1986. Coded 'EH' it was to be sent to the Gulf as the first cadre of aircraft for Operation Granby. As a consequence it received the desert-pink ARTF colour scheme in August 1990 but it had returned to the UK before hostilities began. It received stage three modifications and was painted in ARTF grey in

June 1993 for UN peacekeeping duties and was upgraded to GR.1B standard at St Athan between 13 October 1995 and 22 January 1996. Repainted in the new grey colour scheme in August 1996 it remained with No. 6 Squadron as 'EH' and was later upgraded to GR.3A in January 2002. It went to St Athan for a major overhaul between 30 April and 15 December 2004 and returned to No. 6 Squadron until disbandment. XX970 undertook its last flight on 13 June 2007 to RAF Cosford where it is now in use as a ground instructional airframe.

XX971

S93 F/F 11 December 1975 (R. Stock) and D/D to RAF Bruggen 6 January 1976 for No. 31 Squadron, taking the code 'DE' by June 1976. Repainted into all-over wraparound camouflage at No. 5 MU in November 1976 it was lost in a crash at Lahr, West Germany on 21 March 1978. The fuselage was recovered and dispatched to the AWRE at the PEE, Shoeburyness by December 1979 and was still extant two years later.

XX972

S94 F/F 12 December 1975 (E. Bucklow) and D/D to RAF Bruggen 6 January 1976 for No. 31 Squadron, adopting the code 'DF' by June 1976. It was lost in a crash at Barnard Castle, County Durham during Exercise Osex 4 on 14 April 1981 with the pilot being killed.

XX973

S95 F/F 5 January 1976 (E. Bucklow) and D/D to RAF Bruggen 15 January 1976 for No. 31 Squadron, adopting code 'DG' by June 1976. The aircraft was lost in a crash 4 miles south-west of Gütersloh, West Germany on 14 April 1981 with the pilot ejecting safely.

XX974

S96 F/F 9 January 1976 (E. Bucklow) and D/D to RAF Bruggen 28 January 1976 for No. 31 Squadron where it had taken the code 'DH' by June 1976. It was returned to the UK on 26 October 1984 and, following overhaul, issued to No. 6 Squadron as 'EG'. It was upgraded to GR.1A at JMU in April 1987 returning to No. 6 Squadron. XX974 was part of the first batch of Jaguars to head for the Gulf in August 1990, receiving the ARTF desert-pink colour scheme; however, it returned before hostilities began. Repainted by June 1991 it was later transferred to No. 54 Squadron by January 1992 as 'GH'. The aircraft received a grey ARTF finish in June 1993 for UN peacekeeping duties and again in June 1994, by which time it had received the stage three modifications. It was reassigned to No. 16 (Reserve) Squadron as 'B' in 1993, where by then it had become a GR.3. The aircraft was recoded 'PB' by February 2001 and upgraded at St Athan to GR.3A in November 2001; it was transferred to No. 41 Squadron as 'FE' by March 2003 when once again it received the ARTF finish. It was dispatched by road to St Athan on 16 December 2004 where it was WFU. It then moved to D. Everett Aero, Sproughton and remained there before being sold to a collector in Baarlo, Netherlands in August 2006.

XX975

S97 F/F 12 January 1976 (E. Bucklow) and fitted with rain-erosion strips on leading edges of wings and tailplane. Used on UHF radio trial D/D to Boscombe Down 30 January 1976 for use by 'A' Squadron. D/D to No. 31 Squadron 28 May 1976 becoming 'DJ' by June 1976. It was transferred to No. 17 Squadron as 'BA' by January 1984 and then to No. 226 OCU as '07' by April 1985. Flown to RAF Shawbury for

storage by March 1986 and assigned to ground instructional training at No. 1 SoTT RAF Halton as 8905M. Delivered by December 1986, on closure of the unit it was transferred to RAF Cosford where it still resides today.

XX976

S98 F/F 13 January 1976 (E. Bucklow) and D/D to RAF Bruggen 28 January 1976 for No. 31 Squadron. Coded 'DK' by June 1976. It was transferred to No. 17 Squadron as 'BD' by June 1984 before being retired to RAF Shawbury on 12 March 1985. Assigned to ground instructional duties at No. 1 SoTT by December 1986, it took the maintenance serial 8906M. The aircraft was finally transferred to RAF Cosford on closure of the unit where it still resides today.

XX977

S99 F/F 20 January 1976 (E. Bucklow) and D/D to RAF Bruggen 20 February 1976 for No. 31 Squadron. Coded 'DL' by June 1976 it incurred a bird strike in late April 1978 necessitating attention with No. 431 MU. Flying again on 15 January 1979 it next had an in-flight emergency after it had clipped a tower at Charwelton near Northampton. The aircraft made an emergency landing at RAE Thurleigh having suffered damage to the port wing and external tank. Taken by road to RAF Shawbury on 6 December 1984 it was placed in store until assigned to ground instructional training on 6 December 1991. Initially destined to go to RAF Abingdon for BDR training, it was reallocated to the Aircraft Recovery and Transportation Flight at St Athan until at least January 2006 when Dick Everett at Sproughton acquired it. The nose section was sold to a collector in Boronia, Melbourne, Australia in November 2011 while the fuselage still resides at Sproughton.

XX978

S100 F/F 22 January 1976 (P. Ginger) and D/D to RAF Bruggen 25 February 1976 for No. 31 Squadron taking the code 'DM' by June 1976. The aircraft was lost in a crash on 14 June 1977 near to Verden, West Germany.

XX979

S101 F/F 27 January 1976 (E. Bucklow) and D/D to Boscombe Down 11 February 1976 for use by 'A' Squadron A&AEE. Demonstrated to the president of Romania at Filton on 15 June 1978 it was returned to Warton for EMC checks on 24 January 1979. The jet was then delivered to Farnborough on 30 August 1980. Upgraded to GR.1A standard it was delivered to St Athan for storage in September 1999 where it remained until taken by road to RAF Coltishall on 19 February 2002. Allocated the maintenance serial 9306M, the forward fuselage was to be used as a ground-procedures trainer. In September 2005 it was being used for spares recovery prior to disposal. The nose section went to the Neatishead museum in 2009 where it still resides.

Sporting the No. 41 Squadron farewell markings, XZ103 is seen taking off in torrential weather at RAF Coltishall on 1 April 2006 for the final fly-past before delivery to its new home at RAF Coningsby. The jet was transferred to No. 6 Squadron and undertook its final flight on 12 June 2007 when delivered to RAF Cosford.

XZ101

S102 F/F 4 February 1976 (P. Ginger) and originally incorrectly assigned the serial XY101. D/D to RAF Laarbruch 26 February 1976 for No. 2 (AC) Squadron where it took the code letter 'S'. Repainted into the all-over wraparound colour scheme at No. 5 MU in October 1976 it was later recoded '21' in August 1981 and then transferred to No. 17 Squadron in August 1982 as 'BD'. It returned to No. 2 (AC) Squadron on 10 July 1984 as a GR.1A and coded '20' and then went back to the UK on 7 May 1986 and assigned to No. 41 Squadron as 'Q', becoming the first GR.1A for that unit. The jet remained on strength until early 1993 when transferred to No. 226 OCU as '06' then No. 16 (Reserve) Squadron as 'D' in

March 1994. Placed in store at RAF Coltishall in July 1996 it was later relegated to ground instructional duties as 9282M at Boscombe Down. It was scrapped in 2003.

XZ102

S103 F/F 11 February 1976 (A. Love) and originally incorrectly assigned the serial XY102. D/D RAF Laarbruch 5 March 1976 for No. 2 (AC) Squadron, code 'H'. The aircraft was lost in a crash on 14 December 1976 10km north-east of Laarbruch.

XZ103

S104 F/F 16 February 1976 (E. Bucklow) and originally incorrectly assigned the serial XY103.

D/D to RAF Laarbruch 27 February 1976 for No. 2 (AC) Squadron as code 'I'. It was recoded '23' by August 1980 and upgraded to GR.1A on 3 January 1985. It returned to JMU and then had a brief period in store at RAF Shawbury between November 1990 and June 1992 when it was reissued to No. 41 Squadron as 'P'. It received an arctic ARTF scheme in February 1995 for participation in Exercise Strong Resolve and then went back to St Athan between 18 May and 27 August 1998 when it was upgraded to Jaguar 96 configuration. Returning to No. 41 Squadron it was coded 'FP' then on 23 November 1998, following a multiple bird strike over Herburn, the pilot had to make an emergency landing at Newcastle Airport with one engine shut down and an insecure external tank. The aircraft departed by road to St Athan for repairs but returned to service in January 2000, by which time it had been redesignated GR.3A. The jet was loaned to SAOEU in early 1992 to participate in the annual series of trials held at China Lake NWC. One of these was 'Trial Flashman' which, alongside Tornado GR.4 ZD792, was painted in a mixed ARTF scheme of grey body and undersides and desert-pink upper surfaces. Alas, it went technical just prior to departure and was replaced by XZ109 in normal grey scheme. The special scheme was removed by May 1992 and in 2005 it became the season's Jaguar display platform with No. 41 Squadron. Transferred to No. 6 Squadron as 'FP' in March 2006 it was recoded as 'EF' by February 2007 and undertook its last flight on 12 June 2007 to RAF Cosford to become a ground instructional airframe.

XZ104

S105 F/F 25 February 1976 (J.J. Lee) and originally incorrectly assigned the serial XY104. D/D to

RAF Laarbruch 11 March 1976 for No. 2 (AC) Squadron as code 'N'. It was flown from JMU to Warton on 18 March 1980 for radio trials in conjunction with RAE Farnborough. Recoded '24', the aircraft was selected to receive the unit's special 75th anniversary marks in May 1988. Transferred to No. 6 Squadron on 12 January 1989 it was one of the first aircraft to receive the ARTF desert-pink scheme in March 1989 for a deployment to the Canary Islands. Later it transferred to No. 41 Squadron as 'M' and again received the desert-pink ARTF as a spare aircraft for Operation Granby with the code 'FM'. The aircraft was to receive the stage three modifications and participated in a number of UN peacekeeping operations sporting the grey ARTF. Upgraded to GR.1A and loaned to the SAOEU in August 1996, the aircraft remained on No. 41 strength as 'FM' until flown to RAF Cosford on 27 October 2005 for instructional duties.

Jaguar GR.3 XZ108 'A'

XZ105

S106 F/F 13 February 1976 (E. Bucklow) and originally incorrectly assigned the serial XY105. D/D to RAF Laarbruch 5 March 1976 for No. 2 (AC) Squadron as 'Y'. Recoded '25' by August 1980, it was lost in a crash near to CFB Goose Bay on 16 June 1983 following a collision with XZ110.

XZ106

S107 F/F 23 February 1976 (E. Bucklow) and originally incorrectly assigned the serial XY106. D/D to RAF Laarbruch 5 March 1976 for No. 2 (AC) Squadron as code 'E'. It was recoded '26' in August 1980 and upgraded to GR.1A in August 1984. The jet was flown to RAF Shawbury, by way of Coltishall, on 11 January 1989 for a period of short-term store before delivery to JMU in August 1990 for Gulf War modifications and painting in ARTF desert-pink. It was sent to Thumrait on 6 December 1990 receiving the 'Girl with the Union Jack' nose art, code 'O' and thirty-five mission symbols. It was returned to the UK on 13 March 1991 to No. 41 Squadron as 'FR' but retained the desert-pink scheme. It was then dispatched to Incirlik as part of Operation Warden on 4 September 1991 – a duty it continued to undertake due to its stage three modifications. Loaned to the AWC/SAOEU at Boscombe Down in November 1995 it was redesignated GR.1B or GR.1B®. It went to St Athan on 8 February 2002 for overhaul and GR.3A upgrade. The aircraft was returned to No. 41 Squadron on 12 December 2002 and painted in ARTF snow camouflage for the annual deployment to Bardufoss. It was assigned the code 'FW' in the shuffle post, with No. 16 and No. 54 Squadrons disbanding, but was sent to St Athan in July 2005 for spares recovery. It went to the former RAF Bentwaters by August 2006 until it was sold to the Manston museum by February 2010 where it still resides.

XZ107

S108 F/F 5 March 1976 (E. Bucklow) and originally incorrectly assigned the serial XY107. D/D to RAF Laarbruch 18 March 1976 for No. 2 (AC) Squadron as 'R'. It was recoded '27' then transferred to No. 6 Squadron as 'EN' by December 1982 and on to No. 41 Squadron as 'H' by November 1983. It received an arctic camouflage scheme for deployment

XZ109 seen over the North Sea during the Queen's birthday fly-past practice in 2006. Less than a year later the aircraft had been placed into store at RAF Shawbury.

to Bardufoss between 5 March and 18 March 1988 and again in February 1996 for Exercise Battle Griffin. Upgraded to GR.3 in mid 1997 and GR.3A in November 2003 it remained on No. 41 Squadron strength as 'FH' until WFU at St Athan in March 2006. It went to the former RAF Bentwaters by August 2006 and was last noted in July 2013.

XZ108

S109 F/F 3 March 1976 (J.J. Lee) and originally incorrectly assigned the serial XY108. It was the first aircraft to receive factory-finish wraparound camouflage. It undertook radio trials with XX975. D/D to RAF Laarbruch 9 June 1976 for No. 2 (AC) Squadron as code 'W'. The jet was involved in a landing mishap at De Peel in 1978 and dispatched to No. 431 MU for repairs. It returned to the squadron on 24 August 1979 and was recoded '28'. The aircraft was upgraded to GR.1A by August 1984 and transferred to No. 54 Squadron as 'GD' on 5 January 1989. The jet was involved in a collision with Tornado GR.1A ZA394 'I' of No. 2 (AC) Squadron over Hexham, Northumberland on 9 January 1990. The Jaguar recovered with approximately 1.5m of wing missing, the Tornado crashed although the crew ejected safely. It was repaired at JMU and returned to the squadron but it was reassigned to No. 16 (Reserve) Squadron by February 1994 and coded 'E'. Loaned to A&AEE in February 1995 and received new grey colour scheme at JMU in June 1995, following which it returned to No. 16 (Reserve) Squadron this time as 'A'. It was back with No. 54 Squadron on 8 August 1996 as 'GL' before upgrade to Jaguar 96 configuration at St Athan in January 1998. The aircraft was lost in a crash on 3 September 1998 approximately

12 miles off Norfolk coast during ACM although the pilot ejected safely.

XZ109

S110 F/F 16 March 1976 (P. Ginger) and originally incorrectly assigned serial XY109. D/D 2 April 1976 to RAF Laarbruch for No. 2 (AC) Squadron as 'O'. It was recoded '29' by August 1980 and upgraded at JMU to GR.1A in October 1984. Transferred to RAF Coltishall on 16 December 1988 and after overhaul with the JMU it was assigned to No. 54 Squadron as 'GL' on 13 April 1989. It later received a desert-pink ARTF scheme and was deployed to Incirlik under Operation Warden on 9 September 1991. The jet was then transferred to No. 6 Squadron as 'EN' by March 1993 and, having received the stage three modifications, was used extensively on UN peacekeeping operations in the ARTF grey scheme. Receiving a new, permanent grey scheme in October 1995 it was then upgraded to GR.3 in late 1998 and GR.3A in March 2003 when it was loaned to the SAOEU, although it still remained on No. 6 Squadron strength as 'EN' until at least April 2006. Noted at RAF Shawbury in March 2007, it was later moved to RAF Cosford by August 2009 for instructional duties.

XZ110

S111 F/F 22 March 1976 (A. Love) and originally incorrectly assigned serial XY110. D/D to RAF Laarbruch 5 April 1976 for No. 2 (AC) Squadron as 'J'. Recoded '30' in August 1980 it was later lost in a crash on 16 June 1983 at CFB Goose Bay following a collision with XZ105.

XZ111

S112 F/F 22 March 1976 (E. Bucklow) and originally incorrectly assigned serial XY111.

Glistening after a torrential downpour XZ112 was to be the final aircraft to depart RAF Coltishall.

However, XZ112 was to join a number of its colleagues in store at RAF Shawbury. Here it is still sporting the RAF Coltishall 65th-anniversary colour scheme. By 2009 it had been moved to RAF Cosford for ground instructional duties.

Originally delivered to No. 41 Squadron in April 1976 XZ113's career saw it serve predominantly within the tactical reconnaissance community until delivery to the SAOEU in August 2003, whose markings can be seen here.

D/D to RAF Laarbruch 7 April 1976 for No. 2 (AC) Squadron as code 'A'. Recoded '31' by August 1980 it was transferred to No. 6 Squadron on 27 January 1989 as 'EL'. Received desert-pink ARTF scheme in December 1992 and had gained the inscription 'Thunderbird 1' on nose. Reassigned to No. 54 Squadron as 'GO' it was dispatched to RAF Shawbury for a period of short-term store on 7 September 1993 until given an overhaul at St Athan in October 1995. Resprayed into new grey colour scheme in July 1996 it returned to No. 54 Squadron as 'GO' but was lost in a crash on 27 October 2000 some 5 miles north-east of Dumfries following a bird strike.

XZ112

S113 F/F 22 March 1976 (A. Love) and originally incorrectly assigned serial XY112. D/D to RAF Laarbruch 12 April 1976 for No. 2 (AC) Squadron as code 'G'. Recoded '32' it was upgraded to GR.1A at JMU in November 1982 and flown to RAF Shawbury for short-term store in January 1989. Following overhaul by JMU and stage three modifications it was delivered to RAF Coltishall in February 1991 and received 75th-anniversary markings for No. 54 Squadron. Assigned the code 'GA' it received the grey ARTF scheme in June 1993 and again in September 1994 for UN peacekeeping operations. Repainted into a new grey colour scheme in December 1995 it was upgraded to GR.3 at St Athan in October 1999 and GR.3A in June 2001. It received No. 54 Squadron 89th-anniversary markings in January 2005 and in the post-disbandment shuffle was assigned to No. 41 Squadron as 'FE', but on 29 June 2005 received a special RAF Coltishall 65th-anniversary scheme instead. Although still nominally on No. 41 Squadron strength it

sported the code 'GW' on the NWD. Placed into store at RAF Shawbury between April 2006 and March 2007 it had arrived at RAF Cosford for instructional duties by August 2009.

XZ113

S114 F/F 2 April 1976 (A. Love) and originally incorrectly assigned serial XY113. D/D to RAF Coltishall 27 April 1976 for No. 41 Squadron code 'A'. It was the first aircraft in January 1983 to receive modified squadron markings of white outlined sidebars and red white and red fin band passing through the white outlined code. It was loaned to No. 2 (AC) Squadron as '30' by August 1983 and upgraded to GR.1A on 20 February 1985. The aircraft transferred to No. 54 Squadron as 'GA' in January 1989 and back to No. 41 Squadron as 'D' in August 1989. It received desert-pink ARTF scheme as a spare aircraft for Operation Granby with the code 'FD'. It undertook a number of UN peacekeeping operations in 1993 sporting the grey ARTF scheme and had by this time received the stage three modifications. Painted in desert-pink ARTF for Exercise Jagged Sphinx in December 1996 it was upgraded to GR.3 in mid 1998 and GR.3A in March 2003. The aircraft was loaned to SAOEU in August 2003 although still on No. 41 Squadron strength as code 'FD'. It was sent to St Athan in April 2006 where it was WFU before passing to the former RAF Bentwaters in August 2006, and was last noted there in July 2013.

XZ114

S115 F/F 8 April 1976 (E. Bucklow) and originally incorrectly assigned serial XY114. D/D to RAF Coltishall 6 May 1976 for No. 41 Squadron as code 'B'. It received an arctic ARTF scheme for deployment to Bardufoss in February 1986,

desert-pink ARTF with code 'FB' in March 1993 and ARTF grey in June 1993, but returned to normal camouflage as 'B' in January 1994 only to receive the ARTF desert-pink again in June 1994. Dispatched to RAF Shawbury for storage on 12 December 1994 it remained at that location until transported by road to St Athan on 10 April 2003 for overhaul and upgrading to GR.3A standard. It was reissued to No. 41 Squadron as 'FB' on 5 May 2004, but in the post-disbandment shuffle was assigned to No. 6 Squadron as 'EO' to RAF Shawbury for store in April 2006 until at least March 2007 before transfer to RAF Cosford for instructional duties by August 2009.

XZ115

S116 F/F 30 April 1976 (E. Bucklow) and originally incorrectly assigned serial XY115. D/D to RAF Coltishall 4 June 1976 for No. 41 Squadron code 'C'. Upgraded to GR.1A at JMU in June 1986 it was loaned to No. 2 (AC) Squadron as '23' on 23 August 1988 but was back with No. 41 Squadron again as 'C' on 26 January 1989. It received an arctic camouflage scheme for a deployment to Bardufoss in February 1990 and then painted in desert-pink ARTF for Operation Granby and coded 'FC'. Dispatched to RAF Shawbury for short-term storage in August 1994 it then went by road to St Athan via Coltishall on 5 December 1995. Overhauled and repainted into a new grey scheme it returned to No. 41 Squadron as 'FC' having been redesignated GR.1B. Loaned to SAOEU in January 1997 it was transferred to No. 16 (Reserve) Squadron by December 2001 as 'PD' by which time it was designated a GR.3. In the disbandment reshuffle it was upgraded again to GR.3A at St Athan in December 2004 and assigned to No. 6 Squadron as 'ER'.

The jet went to RAF Shawbury for store in July 2006 but was reassigned to RAF Cosford for instructional duties by October 2006.

XZ116

S117 F/F 22 April 1976 (P. Ginger) and originally incorrectly assigned serial XY116. D/D to RAF Coltishall 28 May 1976 for No. 41 Squadron code 'D'. It received an experimental blue and white ARTF camouflage scheme for Exercise Teamwork at Bardufoss in March 1984. It was upgraded to GR.1A at the JMU in November 1986 but was lost in a crash on 17 June 1987 when it collided head-on with Tornado GR.1 ZA493 'GH' of No. 20 Squadron in Barrowdale Valley, Cumbria with the loss of the pilot. This accident led to the introduction of flow routes in the low-flying areas.

XZ117

S118 F/F 29 April 1976 (A. Love) and originally incorrectly assigned serial XY117. D/D to RAF Coltishall 28 May 1976 for No. 41 Squadron code 'E'. Upgraded to GR.1A at JMU in January 1987 it was later recoded 'P' in late 1990. It was transferred to No. 54 Squadron as 'GG' in April 1991 and received a desert-pink ARTF scheme for Operation Warden in late 1992 and an arctic camouflage in June 1994. Flown to RAF Shawbury for short-term store on 12 July 1994 it was removed by road to RAF Coltishall on 5 December 1995 and then onto St Athan on 10 July 1996 for overhaul and upgrade to GR.3 standard. Reissued to No. 6 Squadron as 'EP' it was back at St Athan on 10 July 2001 for upgrading to GR.3A and the Adour 106 re-engining. F/F in this configuration was in June 2002 and it was

returned to No. 6 Squadron. Received an ARTF scheme in February 2003 for Gulf War II (also known as the Iraq War) but not deployed and returned to the standard new grey scheme by June 2003. In the disbandment reshuffle it was allocated to No. 41 Squadron as 'FB'. The jet was reassigned to No. 6 Squadron as 'ES' in April 2006, remaining as such until just before the squadron disbanded in March 2007. Flown to Boscombe Down on 7 February 2007 as 'Gauntlet 14' where it remained on charge of Qinetq until taken to RAF Cosford on 17 November 2009.

XZ118

S119 F/F 12 May 1976 (D. Eagles) and originally incorrectly assigned serial XY118. D/D to RAF Coltishall 24 May 1976 for No. 41 Squadron as 'F'. Upgraded to GR.1A at JMU in October 1986 it was to receive Gulf War modifications and the ARTF desert-pink scheme before being deployed to Thumrait on 2 November 1990. Named *Buster Gonad* with the code 'Y' on NWD it returned to the UK on 13 March 1991 sporting thirty-eight mission symbols. Retaining the ARTF scheme but coded 'FF' it was one of the first eight jets to be deployed to Incirlik under Operation Warden on 4 September 1991. Having received the stage three modifications it was used extensively on UN peacekeeping operations, receiving the ARTF grey scheme in June 1993 and July 1996 with the application of the new permanent grey scheme in January 1997. Upgraded to GR.3 at St Athan in late 1998 and GR.3A in April 2004 it was assigned the code 'FR' in the disbandment reshuffle. WFU at St Athan in March 2006 it was sold to Dick Everett and placed in store at the former RAF Bentwaters. Fiona Banner acquired it for her art display at the Tate

Modern in December 2010. It was then sold to the Slimelight Club, Islington in April 2011 but subsequently scrapped.

XZ119

S120 F/F 18 May 1976 (P. Ginger) and originally incorrectly assigned serial XY119. D/D to RAF Coltishall 28 May 1976 for No. 41 Squadron code 'G'. Loaned to ETPS in January 1982 it was to receive Gulf War modifications and desert-pink ARTF scheme for deployment to Thumrait on 23 October 1990. Given the nose art 'Katrina Jane' and the code 'Z' on the NWD, it returned to the UK on 12 March 1991 with forty mission symbols, returning to No. 41 Squadron as 'FG'. The jet was one of the first eight aircraft to deploy to Incirlik as part of Operation Warden on 4 September 1991. In spite of later returning to normal camouflage it retained its nose art and mission symbols until at least March 1993. WFU and stored at RAF Coltishall pending disposal; in June 1996 it was taken by road to RAF Cranwell for ground instructional duties as 9266M where it remained until at least August 2006. By August 2009 it had been sold to the museum at East Fortune where it resides today.

XZ120

S121 F/F 19 May 1976 (P. Ginger) and originally incorrectly assigned serial XY120. D/D to RAF Laarbruch 15 June 1976 for No. 2 (AC) Squadron as code '20'; it was lost in a crash off Nordholm, Denmark on 25 February 1977. The wreck was recovered and disposed of to Park Aviation Supply, Faygate, Sussex.

XZ355

S122 F/F 10 June 1976 (E. Bucklow) and D/D RAF Coltishall 8 July 1976 for No. 41 Squadron, code 'H'. It was transferred to No. 54 Squadron as 'GA' on 14 April 1982 but back to No. 41 Squadron as 'J' on 9 March 1984. It was upgraded to GR.1A at JMU in August 1986 and noted sporting a stripped arctic camouflage for deployment to Bardufoss in February 1990. Receiving a desert-pink ARTF scheme in August 1990 for Operation Granby it was coded 'FJ' in January 1991. It was deployed to Incirlik on Operation Warden duties on 4 September 1991 having received the stage three modifications. It was returned to No. 41 Squadron 'J' by February 1995, only to receive arctic camouflage for Exercise Strong Resolve the same month. Loaned to Boscombe Down in July 1996 as a GR.1A, the jet received the new grey camouflage scheme at St Athan on 7 October 1997. Upgraded to GR.3 in October 1998 and GR.3A in August 2001 it remained on No. 41 Squadron strength as code 'FJ' until WFU at St Athan in April 2006. Sold to Dick Everett it was moved to the former RAF Bentwaters before being sold to a private collector in Greece. There was a report of the airframe being impounded at Acona in January 2009.

XZ356

S123 F/F 7 June 1976 (E. Bucklow) and D/D to RAF Coltishall 9 July 1976 for No. 41 Squadron as code 'J'. After incurring a bird strike it was placed in short-term store at the JMU by September 1978. It was repaired and reissued to No. 17 Squadron as 'BP' on 27 October 1980. Recoded 'BJ' by April 1984 it was then transferred to No. 14 Squadron as 'AU' by April 1985. The aircraft went to JMU for upgrade to GR.1A and was issued to No. 41 Squadron again as 'J' on 24 February 1986. It was recoded 'R' post overhaul in August 1990 and painted in desert-pink ARTF camouflage as spare aircraft for Operation Granby. Upgraded with Gulf War modifications it was deployed to Thumrait on 2 November 1990 where it received 'Mary Rose' nose art and the code 'N' on the NWD. It returned to the UK on 12 March 1991 with thirty-three mission symbols. Reassigned to No. 6 Squadron as 'EP' it had lost its desert-pink scheme by October 1992 only to have it reapplied the following month. Repainted in ARTF grey by June 1993 for UN peacekeeping operations it was dispatched to St Athan in August 1997, only to be redirected to RAF Shawbury for storage. It remained in storage until 9 March 2001 when it was taken back to St Athan by road for overhaul and upgrade. Issued to No. 54 Squadron on 30 May 2002 as a GR.3A and coded 'GF' it was immediately loaned to SAOEU for a month. It was reassigned to No. 41 Squadron and allocated code 'FU' in the disbandment shuffle. WFU at St Athan in March 2006 it was sold to Dick Ecerett at the former RAF Bentwaters. Noted for sale on eBay in November 2006 it is now on display in Welshpool.

XZ357

S124 F/F 17 June 1976 (A. Love) and D/D to RAF Coltishall 16 July 1976 for No. 41 Squadron as code 'K'. It underwent engine upgrade in June 1978 becoming the first aircraft to receive dash-26 engines. Later received light blue/grey arctic scheme for Exercise Alloy Express in early 1982. It moved to JMU on 2 January 1986 for GR.1A upgrade and overhaul, returning to the unit as 'K'. Although it received the desert-pink ARTF scheme for Operation Granby it did not participate in hostilities and had returned to standard camouflage by April 1991. It then received ARTF grey for UN peacekeeping operations in July 1993 then, whilst on overhaul at St Athan, it became the first Jaguar to receive the new permanent grey scheme in February 1995. It was upgraded to Jaguar 96 in February 1999 with No. 41 Squadron as 'FK' then GR.3A at St Athan in September 1901. It was WFU by October 2004 with the fuselage, minus the cockpit section, dispatched to St Athan for spares reclamation on 28 October 2004. Noted noseless at Sproughton in October 2005 it had later been sold to a collector in Kessel by February 2010. It was stored at Baarlo in November 2015.

XZ358

S125 F/F 25 June 1976 (E. Bucklow) and fitted with dash-26 engines for demonstration at the 1976 SBAC show. D/D to RAF Coltishall 2 November 1976 for No. 41 Squadron as code 'L'. The aircraft suffered a ground fire on 21 February 1977 but was repaired and noted sporting the light blue and grey arctic camouflage for Exercise Alloy Express in early 1982. It received similar treatment in March 1985 for another deployment to Norway before upgrading to GR.1A. In 1990 the jet received Gulf War modifications and the desert-pink ARTF colour scheme and deployed to Thumrait on 23 October 1990 where it received the nose art 'Diplomatic Service' and the code 'W' on the NWD. It returned to the UK on 13 March 1991 with fourteen mission symbols. Coded 'FL' it retained its desert-pink scheme and was deployed to Incirlik on 4 September 1991 under Operation Warden. It remained with the squadron, receiving ARTF schemes in support of UN peacekeeping operations until WFU at RAF Coltishall in July 1996. Reassigned to ground instructional duties it was dispatched to RAF Cranwell on 15 October 1996 for use by the Aircraft Maintenance Instruction Flight

as 9262M where it remained in use until the flight relocated to RAF Cosford. It was current in November 2013.

XZ359

S126 F/F 8 July 1976 (E. Bucklow) and D/D to RAF Coltishall 25 August 1976 for No. 41 Squadron as code 'M'. The aircraft received the light blue and grey arctic scheme for Exercise Alloy Express in 1982 and was upgraded to GR.1A at the JMU in July 1986. Once again it deployed to Bardufoss sporting an arctic scheme in January 1989, but it was lost in a crash on 13 April 1989 when it struck cliffs at St Abbs Head, Berwick killing the pilot.

XZ360

S127 F/F 14 September 1976 (R. Stock) and D/D to RAF Abingdon 31 August 1976 for storage. Issued to No. 41 Squadron on 29 April 1977 as 'Y' it was recoded 'N' on 8 February 1984 and upgraded to GR.1A at the JMU in July 1986. It received stage three modifications to allow overseas UN peacekeeping operations and received the code 'FN' and an ARTF grey scheme in September 1994, August 1995 and January 1997. Upgraded to Jaguar 96 at St Athan in September 1998, it was redesignated GR.3 in September 2000. GR.3A modifications came in February 2003 and the jet was painted in ARTF again for Gulf War II but never deployed. Returning to a standard scheme by May 2003 it was assigned the code 'FN'. WFU at St Athan in March 2006 and sold to Dick Everett at the former RAF Bentwaters by August 2006; it was still current in July 2013.

XZ361

S128 F/F 4 August 1976 (R. Stock) and D/D to RAF Abingdon 2 September 1976 for storage. Issued

to No. 2 (AC) Squadron as 'II' on 16 March 1977, it was recoded '20' by August 1980 and '25' by July 1983. Upgraded to GR.1A at the JMU in February 1985 it was returned to the unit but then flown to RAF Shawbury by January 1989 for short-term storage. Overhauled at St Athan in September 1992 it was issued to No. 41 Squadron taking the code 'T'. It received an arctic scheme for Exercise Battle Griffin in February 1995 and again in March 1996. Recoded 'FT' it was upgraded to GR.3 at St Athan in 2000 but was flown to RAF Shawbury again on 26 June 2002 for storage where it has remained until it was put up for disposal by tender DSAT 3146 on 26 May 2005. It was sold to Dick Everett Aero, Sproughton, Suffolk and departed for its new home on 15 December 2005. The aircraft is now displayed at the former USAFE base at Bentwaters.

XZ362

S129 F/F 19 August 1976 (A. Love) and displayed at 1976 SBAC show. D/D 27 September 1976 to RAF Abingdon prior to delivery to No. 2 (AC) Squadron. Taking the code '19' by August 1980 and then '27' by January 1982, it was transferred to No. 41 Squadron as code 'E' on 25 May 1990 followed by No. 54 Squadron as 'GC' in April 1993. It received ARTF grey scheme for UN peacekeeping duties in June 1993 and again in September 1994. It received the stage three modifications and became the first No. 54 Squadron aircraft to receive the new permanent grey scheme on 23 January 1996. It was lost in a crash on 24 July 1996 during Dissimilar Air Combat Training (DACT), whilst participating in exercise Cope Thunder in Alaska, with the No. 41 Squadron pilot ejecting safely.

XZ363

S130 F/F 25 August 1976 (J.J. Cockburn) and D/D to RAF Abingdon 14 September 1976 for storage. Issued to No. 41 Squadron by August 1977 as code 'Z', it was recoded 'A' by September 1983 and upgraded to GR.1A at the JMU in October 1986. The jet was painted in a special anniversary colour scheme in March 1990 of a red fin containing a white flash with the cross of Lorraine at the top. Later, in August 1990, it received the desert-pink ARTF scheme for Operation Granby but did not participate in hostilities. Coded 'FA' by January 1991 and then 'FO' in June 1991 it had retained its ARTF finish before returning to normal camouflage by October 1992. The desert-pink scheme was applied once again in November 1992 for a period of UN peacekeeping duties but in May 1993 it received a white and green arctic scheme. It was flown to RAF Shawbury by October 1995 for a period of short-term store then went to St Athan for overhaul emerging on 13 November 1996 as a GR.1B and in the new grey colour scheme when loaned to Boscombe Down. It then returned to No. 41 Squadron as 'FO' as a GR.3. It was lost in a crash on 25 July 2001 whilst being flown by a No. 54 Squadron pilot during Exercise Cope Thunder.

XZ364

S131 F/F 3 September 1976 (R.J. Stock) and D/D to RAF Abingdon 27 September 1976 for storage. Issued to No. 2 (AC) Squadron by August 1980 as '18' but recoded '21' by January 1983. It was upgraded to GR.1A at JMU in February 1985 and transferred to No. 54 Squadron as 'GJ' in January 1989. The aircraft received Gulf War modifications and the desert-pink colour scheme and deployed to Thumrait on 23 October 1990. Here it received the 'Sadman'

nose art and the code 'Q' on the NWD. Returned to UK on 1 March 1991 with forty-seven mission marks and repainted into standard camouflage by June 1991. ARTF grey was applied in June 1993 and again in September 1994. In 1996 after a period of loan at Boscombe Down and overhaul at St Athan the jet was repainted into the new grey colour scheme. Reported as both a GR.1B and GR.1B (T) it was upgraded to GR.3 at St Athan in May 1999 and later to GR.3A. It received special RAF Coltishall 60th-anniversary markings on 29 June 2000, and following the disbandment of No. 54 Squadron was reassigned to No. 41 Squadron as 'FS' in the resulting reshuffle. WFU at St Athan in March 2006 it had been sold to Dick Everett at Sproughton by August 2007. The nose section was later sold to a private collector in 2010 in the Royal Tunbridge Wells area.

XZ365

S132 F/F 19 September 1976 (E. Bucklow) and D/D to RAF Abingdon 1 October 1976 for storage. Issued to No. 41 Squadron as 'D' by September 1977, it was recoded 'J' by June 1979 and became the first squadron aircraft to receive modified unit insignia with previous red markings outlined in white. It became the third aircraft to receive the avionics update to GR.1A standard and the second to be outshopped by the JMU on 9 March 1984. It was reassigned to No. 54 Squadron as 'GC' on 14 March 1984 and then to No. 2 (AC) Squadron as '33' in August 1984. It was then lost in a crash near Meschede, east of Dortmond, West Germany on 9 July 1985.

XZ366

S133 F/F 20 September 1976 (R. Stock) and D/D to RAF Abingdon 6 October 1976 for storage.

Issued to No. 2 (AC) Squadron in 1978 and coded '22' by September 1980, it was upgraded at the JMU in July 1984 to GR.1A standard. Following conversion by No. 2 (AC) Squadron to Tornado GR.1A, the jet was flown to RAF Shawbury for storage in January 1989, remaining there until at least June 1992. Reissued to No. 41 Squadron as 'S' on 4 June 1992 it was involved in visibility trials, flying with white external tanks. It received an arctic scheme in February 1995 when participating in Exercise Strong Resolve and emerged from St Athan on 24 July 1995 sporting the new permanent grey colour scheme. Recoded 'FS' the jet was modified to Jaguar 96 configuration at St Athan in March 1999 then GR.3A in December 2000. In the resulting reshuffle, following the disbandment of No. 16 and No. 54 Squadrons, XZ366 was allocated the code 'FC'. WFU at St Athan in March 2006 it was sold to Everett Aerospace in August 2006 and was last noted at the former RAF Bentwaters in July 2013.

XZ367

S134 F/F 6 October 1976 (E. Bucklow) and D/D to RAF Abingdon 1 November 1976 for storage. Issued to No. 2 (AC) Squadron as 'H' by May 1977, it was returned to store at JMU in January 1978 where it remained until at least June 1980. Reissued to No. 226 OCU as '25' on 30 June 1981 it was upgraded to GR.1A on 31 October 1985 and returned to No. 2 (AC) Squadron as '33' before being recoded '20'. Transferred to No. 54 Squadron as 'GP' on 18 January 1989 it was to receive the Gulf War modifications and desert-pink colour scheme and deployed to Thumrait on 23 October 1990. Here it received the nose art 'Debbie', but later changed to 'White Rose', and the code 'P' on the NWD. It returned to the UK on 13 March

1991 sporting forty mission symbols and had reverted to standard camouflage by May 1991. It was dispatched to JMU on 14 June 1991 for overhaul, becoming the last of its type to be overhauled at Abingdon. Returned to No. 54 Squadron by January 1992, it received stage three modifications at St Athan in July 1994 and a grey ARTF scheme in February 1995 for UN peacekeeping operations. It was returned to desert-pink in November 1996 for Exercise Desert Sphinx and upon return placed in short-term store at RAF Coltishall. Upgraded to GR.3A at St Athan in March 2000 but overstressed during Operation Warden at Incirlik. Returned to Coltishall and then taken by road to RAF Shawbury for storage on 29 September 2000 where it remained until returning to Coltishall on 2 October 2002 in the ground instructional role as the weapon loading training airframe. Whilst in this role it received the No. 6 Squadron anniversary-scheme fin prior to the schemes application on XX112. It was present at the closure of RAF Coltishall but had arrived with Everett Aerospace at Bentwaters by September 2006. However, an embarrassing situation of the MoD having to 'buy back' the airframe occurred in April 2010 and the aircraft is now in instructional use at RAF Cosford.

XZ368

S135 F/F 1 October 1976 (E. Bucklow) and D/D to RAF Bruggen 1 November 1976 for No. 14 Squadron as code 'AN'. It was reassigned to No. 6 Squadron on 11 June 1979 becoming code 'EL', but it had returned to No. 14 Squadron on 7 February 1984 as 'AG' before moving to Coltishall in October 1985. Assigned to ground instructional duties at Cosford on 27 October 1986 it was to receive the maintenance serial 8900M and remains here today.

XZ369

S136 F/F 11 October 1976 (J.J. Lee) and D/D to RAF Bruggen 1 November 1976 for No. 14 Squadron as 'AP'. It was transferred to No. 17 Squadron as 'BF' by October 1983 then sent to RAF Shawbury on 5 March 1985 for short-term storage. Upgraded to GR.1A and issued to No. 6 Squadron as 'EE' on 3 March 1987, it was recoded 'EF' following overhaul at JMU in May 1989. It received the desert-pink ARTF scheme for Operation Granby but did not take part in hostilities. Used on UN peacekeeping operations post Granby, it received the grey ARTF finish in June 1993 and September 1994. Upgraded to GR.1B at St Athan in October 1995 it immediately undertook overseas operations, again sporting the grey ARTF finish. With St Athan on overhaul 21 October 1996 through to 21 August 1997, it was returned to No. 6 Squadron as a Jaguar 96 (T) then in September 2000 upgraded to GR.3A at St Athan. Still assigned to No. 6 Squadron but allocated the code 'EU' in the post-disbandment reshuffle. WFU at St Athan in March 2006 it was sold to Everett Aerospace, arriving at the former RAF Bentwaters by August 2006. It was last noted in July 2013 before being sold to the Delta Force Paintball site at Upminster in 2016.

XZ370

S137 F/F 20 October 1976 (E. Bucklow) and D/D to RAF Bruggen 4 November 1976 for No. 14 Squadron but passed to No. 17 Squadron as 'BN'. It returned to the UK on 20 March 1985 into storage at RAF Shawbury and was assigned to ground instructional training at RAF Cosford. Allocated maintenance serial 9004M and coded 'JB' it had arrived at Cosford by January 2000 where it remains today.

XZ371

S138 F/F 3 November 1976 (E. Bucklow) and D/D to RAF Bruggen 7 December 1976 for No. 17 Squadron as 'BP'. During a NATO exchange with JaBoG.32 it received a JaBoG.32 badge beneath the cockpit with the serial 17+32 and the inscription 'Lechfeld Airlines'. It was recoded 'BB' before being transferred to No. 14 Squadron as 'AP' by August 1984. Flown to RAF Shawbury on 13 December 1985 for storage and assigned to ground instructional training at RAF Cosford. Allocated maintenance serial 8907M, it had arrived by January 2000 where it still resides today.

XZ372

S139 F/F 10 November 1976 (E. Bucklow) and D/D to RAF Bruggen 7 December 1976 for No. 14 Squadron code 'AQ'. Transferred to No. 20 Squadron as 'CB' by October 1983 then reassigned to No. 226 OCU as '04' on 18 January 1984. Upgraded to GR.1A at JMU in September 1985 it was reissued to No. 6 Squadron as 'ED'. Painted in desert-pink ARTF for Operation Granby the jet did not participate in hostilities, but by February 1995 had received the stage three modifications. It was noted sporting an arctic camouflage in February 1995 for participation in Exercise Strong Resolve and later, in September 1996, noted in store at Boscombe Down. Dispatched to St Athan for further storage it remained there until 7 February 2000 when it entered the overhaul and upgrade programme. Reissued to No. 6 Squadron coded 'ED' on 30 November 2000 as a GR.3A, it was transferred to No. 41 Squadron as 'FV' in the disbandment reshuffle but was subsequently WFU at St Athan where it arrived on 5 July 2005. It was sold to Everett Aerospace at the former RAF Bentwaters and then later sold on to the Aberdeen/Dyce Airport fire section on 19 December 2011. It was still extant in April 2013.

XZ373

S140 F/F 19 November 1976 (R. Stock) and D/D to RAF Bruggen 7 December 1976 for No. 17 Squadron as 'BQ'. Recoded 'BB' when dispatched to JMU for overhaul in April 1981 it was later transferred to No. 20 Squadron as 'CG' by November 1983. Flown to RAF Shawbury for short-term store on 14 July 1984 it was returned to JMU in September 1984 for upgrade to GR.1A and was delivered to No. 6 Squadron as 'EC' on 28 January 1985. Reassigned to No. 54 Squadron as 'GF', by June 1988 it was to receive the stage three modifications to permit overseas peacekeeping duties and was noted sporting the grey ARTF in September 1993. Still with No. 54 Squadron it was lost during an ACM sortie over the Adriatic on 26 June 1995, with the USAF exchange pilot ejecting safely. The scrap was reported at RAF Marham for disposal in January 1997.

XZ374

S141 F/F 9 December 1976 (E. Bucklow) and D/D to RAF Bruggen 5 January 1977 for No. 20 Squadron code 'CA'. Transferred to No. 14 Squadron as 'AD' by October 1983 then flown to RAF Shawbury on 13 August 1985 for storage, but allocated to ground instructional duties as 9005M at RAF Cosford. Coded 'JC' with the school it was still in use until August 2011 but was not noted in March 2016.

XZ375

S142 F/F 16 December 1976 (E. Bucklow) and D/D to RAF Bruggen 24 January 1977 for No. 20 Squadron as 'CB'. Reassigned to No. 14 Squadron

as 'AK' by October 1983, it was upgraded at JMU to GR.1A standard in February 1986 and transferred to No. 54 Squadron as 'GB'. It was stored at JMU between 21 September 1987 and 23 October 1990, by which time it had received Gulf War modifications and the desert-pink ARTF colour scheme. Flown to Thumrait on 23 October 1990 it was to receive the nose ARTF 'Guardian Reader' and the code 'S' on the NWD. It returned to the UK on 12 March 1991 sporting seventeen mission symbols and reverted to No. 54 Squadron as 'GR'. It, however, retained its desert-pink ARTF scheme and deployed again on 9 September 1991 to Incirlik on Operation Warden. It later received stage three modifications and the ARTF grey scheme for future UN peacekeeping operations. Overhauled at St Athan in August 1995 it emerged in the new grey scheme and was updated to GR.1B standard. However, it was placed in store and allocated to ground instructional duties as 9255M with the DARA civilian technical training school where it was noted in January 1997. WFU it was dispatched by road to RAF Coltishall on 19 February 2002 when the forward fuselage section was acquired by Mick Jennings for his cockpit collection. This was resprayed into desert-pink and the 'Guardian Reader' inscription put back on with the remainder used for BDRT. The rear fuselage was noted awaiting disposal in September 2005 and the nose section moved to the Norwich Aviation Museum with the remainder of Mick Jennings collection in April 2007 where it is still present.

XZ376

S143 F/F 13 January 1977 (R. Stock) and D/D to RAF Bruggen for No. 14 Squadron as 'AE'. It was transferred to No. 17 Squadron as 'BE' by September 1978 but was lost in a crash on

Tain range, Scotland on 7 March 1983 with the pilot ejecting safely.

XZ377

S144 F/F 21 January 1977 (A. Love) and D/D to RAF Bruggen 15 February 1977 for No. 20 Squadron as code 'CF'. The jet was transferred to No. 31 Squadron as 'DF' by March 1984 and No. 2 (AC) Squadron in November 1984 as code '39'. It went to JMU on 6 February 1985 for overhaul and upgrade to GR.1A before reissue to No. 226 OCU code '02'. The aircraft was transferred to No. 54 Squadron on 11 February 1987 and on to No. 6 Squadron as 'EB' when it received the desert-pink ARTF scheme as a spare aircraft for Operation Granby. It was passed to No. 16 (Reserve) Squadron as 'B' in April 1997 then to St Athan for upgrade to Jaguar 96 configuration, after which it returned to No. 6 Squadron as 'EG'. Noted sporting the ARTF grey scheme in January 2003 for the second Gulf conflict but it was not deployed. Upgraded again at St Athan between 2 April 2004 and 19 January 2005 to GR.3A and allocated code 'EP' in the disbandment reshuffle. WFU at St Athan in April 2006 it was later transferred to RAF Cosford for instructional duties where it is still current.

XZ378

S145 F/F 1 February 1977 (E. Bucklow) and D/D to RAF Bruggen 15 February 1977 for No. 20 Squadron as code 'CH'. It was transferred to No. 31 Squadron as 'DG' by December 1983, to No. 17 Squadron as 'BB' by June 1984 and finally to No. 41 Squadron as 'P' before dispatch to JMU for upgrade to GR.1A in July 1985. Reissued to No. 6 Squadron as 'EP' it was flown to RAF Shawbury in October 1990 for storage where it remained, but was put up for disposal on 26 May 2005 under DSAT 3146. It was sold on 14 November 2005 to a Mr Langdon of Topsham, Exeter with whom it is still currently.

XZ381

S146 F/F 16 February 1977 (E. Bucklow) and D/D to RAF Bruggen 17 March 1977 for No. 20 Squadron code 'CD'. It was transferred to No. 17 Squadron code 'BL' by January 1984 before being flown to RAF Shawbury on 20 March 1985 for storage. It was taken to JMU for overhaul in March 1989 and reissued to No. 54 Squadron as 'GB'. It was painted in desert-pink ARTF and deployed to Incirlik on 9 September 1991 as part of Operation Warden, having received the stage three modifications. It was then transferred to No. 6 Squadron as 'EC' by March 1993 and noted wearing the ARTF grey scheme in June 1993. The aircraft then went to JMU again on 28 June 1994 followed by a period at Boscombe Down for TIALD integration, returning to Coltishall in January 1996, by then designated as GR.1B. It was dispatched to St Athan on 26 July 1996 for modification and painting in the new grey scheme, then again on 10 August 1998 to be brought up to Jaguar 96 standard. Transferred to No. 16 (Reserve) Squadron and allocated the code 'D', it gained an all-black fin with a yellow 'Saint' marking but was lost in a crash on 20 October 1999 6 miles north of RAF Lossiemouth in the Moray Firth. The pilot ejected safely.

XZ382

S147 F/F 10 March 1977 (E. Bucklow) and D/D to RAF Bruggen 6 April 1977 for No. 17 Squadron as 'BE'. It was transferred to No. 14 Squadron as 'AE' by September 1978 and then flown to the JMU in March 1980 where it remained until at least November 1982. It was moved to St Athan by May 1983 and RAF Shawbury by November 1985, at which point it was assigned to the ground instructional role. Allocated maintenance serial 8908M it was dispatched to No. 1 SoTT at RAF Halton by December 1986. Following the closure of the unit it was then taken to RAF Coltishall on 13 October 1992 for BDRT where it remained until at least May 1998 – it has subsequently been passed into the hands of the preservationists at Bruntingthorpe.

XZ383

S148 F/F 11 March 1977 (A. Love) and D/D to RAF Bruggen on 19 April 1977 for No. 17 Squadron code 'BC'. Transferred to No. 14 Squadron as 'AF' by November 1983 it was then flown to RAF Coltishall in October 1985 before being relegated to the ground instructional role. Dispatched to RAF Cosford on 27 October 1986 with maintenance serial 8901M it remains in use as such today.

XZ384

S149 F/F 18 March 1977 (E. Bucklow) and D/D to RAF Bruggen 6 April 1977 for No. 20 Squadron as 'CM'. Reassigned to No. 31 Squadron as 'DG' on 10 July 1984 but passed to No. 17 Squadron as 'BC' in October 1984. It was flown to RAF Shawbury for storage on 28 February 1985 before being assigned to ground instructional duties at No. 2 SoTT RAF Cosford in March 1988. Assigned the maintenance serial 8954M it remains in use at RAF Cosford today.

XZ385

S150 F/F 25 March 1977 (E. Bucklow) and D/D to RAF Bruggen 21 April 1977 for No. 14 Squadron as 'AG'. Recoded 'AA' in October 1982 it was transferred to No. 17 Squadron as 'BE' by

June 1983 prior to dispatch to the JMU in early 1985. Reissued to No. 41 Squadron in April 1985 it was assigned to the 'Gib Det' as 'G' prior to joining No. 6 Squadron as 'EK' in September 1985. Upgraded at JMU to GR.1A in July 1986 then joined No. 54 Squadron as 'GM', but was loaned to Boscombe Down in September 1990 for fitment and trials with over-wing missile rails. The aircraft was transferred to No. 16 (Reserve) Squadron as '03' by September 1993 following overhaul at St Athan. It was recoded 'F' in March 1994 before receiving the new grey colour scheme and the code 'C'. Loaned to No. 6 Squadron before returning to No. 16 (Reserve) Squadron as 'R', it was then sent to St Athan for overhaul and modification to GR.3. The jet returned to No. 16 (Reserve) Squadron as 'C' in August 2000 but was upgraded to GR.3A at St Athan in December 2003 and recoded 'PC'. It was later assigned to No. 41 Squadron as 'FT' following the disbandment reshuffles but was WFU at St Athan in March 2006. It was finally sold to Everett Aerospace at the former RAF Bentwaters where it was last noted in July 2013.

XZ386

S151 F/F 19 April 1977 (E. Bucklow) and D/D to RAF Bruggen, via RAF Coltishall, 16 May 1977 for No. 14 Squadron as 'AJ'. It was transferred to No. 31 Squadron as 'DB' by December 1983 but flown to UK on 24 October 1984 following the unit's transition to Tornado. Reissued to No. 2 (AC) Squadron as '38' but recoded '32' in April 1985. The jet became part of 'Gib Det' as 'B' then reassigned to No. 6 Squadron as 'EK' by October 1985. Upgraded to GR.1A at JMU in December 1985 it was then reassigned to No. 226 OCU as '05' in February 1986.

Unfortunately it crashed on 24 June 1987 into a hillside near Aberedu, Powys, Wales with the loss of the pilot.

XZ387

S152 F/F 6 May 1977 (E. Bucklow) and D/D to RAF Bruggen 26 May 1977 for No. 31 Squadron where it took the code 'DN'. Returned to the UK on 2 November 1984 and upgraded at the JMU to GR.1A and reissued to No. 6 Squadron as 'EB' before transfer to No. 54 Squadron as 'GG' in March 1990. The aircraft crashed on 12 September 1990 into the Solway Firth 5 miles off Southerness Point, Dumfries & Galloway, with the loss of the pilot. In September 1993 the diving vessel *Oliver Felix* recovered its rear section and wing.

XZ388

S153 F/F 12 May 1977 (E. Bucklow) and D/D to RAF Bruggen on 5 June 1977 for No. 17 Squadron as 'BK'. It was transferred to No. 14 Squadron as 'AH' but was lost in a crash near Rebberlah, north-east of Celle, West Germany on 2 April 1985 with the pilot ejecting safely.

XZ389

S154 F/F 7 May 1977 (R. Stock) and D/D to RAF Bruggen 24 June 1977 for No. 20 Squadron as 'CN'. It was transferred to No. 31 Squadron in October 1983 as 'DM' and then to No. 17 Squadron as 'BL' in October 1984. The jet was then flown to RAF Shawbury on 28 February 1985 for storage. Allocated to ground instructional duties at RAF Halton it had arrived with No. 1 SoTT by March 1988 and was assigned maintenance serial 8946M. At the closure of the unit the jet was transferred to RAF Cosford where it still resides today.

XZ390

S155 F/F 9 June 1977 (J.J. Lee) and D/D to RAF Bruggen 5 July 1977 for No. 31 Squadron as 'DM'. Following overhaul at JMU it was reassigned to No. 20 Squadron as 'CL' then transferred to No. 2 (AC) Squadron as '35' by July 1984. Flown to RAF Shawbury on 25 April 1985 for storage it was later assigned to ground instructional duties at No. 2 SoTT RAF Cosford, with maintenance serial 9003M, where it remains today.

XZ391

S156 F/F 23 June 1977 (J.J. Lee) and D/D to RAF Bruggen 15 July 1977 for No. 31 Squadron as 'DP'. Recoded 'DF' on 15 September 1982 it was dispatched to JMU in February 1984 for overhaul and upgrading to GR.1A, following that it was reissued to No. 54 Squadron as 'GE' on 21 June 1984. It was recoded 'GN' after attention at the JMU in April 1987 and then flown to RAF Shawbury for storage on 12 February 1990, but had departed for overhaul at St Athan by February 1991. It was issued to No. 226 OCU as '05' on 21 November 1991 although had returned to No. 54 Squadron as 'GM' by June 1992. In June 1993 it had ARTF grey applied for UN peacekeeping operations and undertook the high-visibility trials with white external tanks in February 1995. Overhaul again at St Athan saw the jet emerge on 1 March 1996 in the new grey colour scheme and it was transferred to No. 16 (Reserve) Squadron as 'A' on 30 July 1996. A return to St Athan beckoned in February 1999 when it was modified to Jaguar 96 standard and on 28 May 1999 it was reassigned to No. 6 Squadron as 'EB'. Upgrade to GR.3A took place in August 2001 and in the post-disbandment reshuffle of both No. 16 and No. 54 Squadrons it was allocated to No. 6

Squadron as 'ET'. It went to RAF Shawbury for store by April 2006 and was later transferred to the DCAE Cosford on 9 March 2007 where it still resides today.

XZ392

S157 F/F 13 July 1977 (D. Eagles) and D/D to RAF Bruggen 17 August 1977 for No. 31 Squadron as 'DQ'. It was recoded 'DE' by June 1979 and transferred to No. 20 Squadron as 'CC' by November 1983 before being handed on to No. 54 Squadron as 'GR' by October 1984. Upgraded to GR.1A at the JMU in June 1987 and returned to No. 54 Squadron as 'GQ'. Flown to RAF Shawbury for storage by October 1990 it remained in a semi-operational state until dispatch to St Athan by road on 1 December 2000 for overhaul and upgrade to GR.3A. Assigned to No. 16 (Reserve) Squadron as 'PF' on 26 March 2002, it received special marks the following year and in the post-disbandment reshuffle was allocated to No. 6 Squadron as 'EM'. Remained with the squadron until disbandment, undertaking its last flight on 12 June 2007 to RAF Cosford for ground instructional duties.

XZ393

S158 F/F 12 August 1977 (E. Bucklow) and D/D to RAF Bruggen 1 September 1977 for No. 20 Squadron as 'CP'. Transferred to No. 17 Squadron as 'BJ' by June 1980, following attention at the JMU it went to No. 226 OCU as '03'. Upgraded in February 1984 to GR.1A and reassigned to No. 54 Squadron as 'GK' it was lost in a crash off Cromer on 12 July 1984.

XZ394

S159 F/F 2 September 1977 (A. Love) and D/D to RAF Bruggen 26 September 1977 for

The penultimate front-line RAF Jaguar to be built, XZ399 took its first flight on 23 November 1977 but was not delivered to the RAF until eighteen months later for use by No. 6 Squadron. Young by RAF standards it served for only twenty-eight years and is seen here in LFA7 just prior to retirement on 12 June 2007.

No. 20 Squadron as 'CQ' before being passed on to No. 17 Squadron as 'BJ'. Flown to RAF Shawbury for short-term storage on 20 March 1985 it was then shipped to the JMU in early 1987 for upgrade to GR.1A and reissued to No. 6 Squadron as 'ES'. Transferred to No. 54 Squadron as 'GN' by March 1990 it was noted sporting the ARTF grey colour scheme in June 1993 and again in September 1994 for UN peacekeeping operations. The jet received the new, permanent grey colour scheme in July 1996, it was then upgraded to GR.3 in October 1998 and finally to GR.3A in November 2001. In the disbandment reshuffle the jet was allocated to No. 41 Squadron as 'FG'. WFU at St Athan in April 2006 it was sold to Everett Aerospace at the former RAF Bentwaters by August 2006, remaining there

until at least July 2012. The aircraft is now preserved at Shoreham Aerodrome.

XZ395
S160 F/F 8 September 1977 (E. Bucklow) and passed into store at Warton. Finally D/D to RAF Coltishall 30 January 1979 for No. 54 Squadron, eventually taking up the code 'GN'. The aircraft was then transferred to No. 6 Squadron as 'EJ' in May 1984. Following upgrade to GR.1A at the JMU in August 1984 it had returned to No. 54 Squadron as 'GJ', only to be lost in a crash 30 miles north of Coltishall on 22 August 1984 with the pilot ejecting successfully.

XZ396
S161 F/F 19 December 1977 (E. Bucklow) and passed into storage at Warton where it was

to remain for over a year before D/D to RAF Coltishall on 23 February 1979. Assigned to No. 6 Squadron it eventually took the code 'EM' but was transferred to No. 226 OCU as '08' by May 1984. Following upgrade to GR.1A at the JMU it was reissued to No. 6 Squadron as 'EM' on 18 February 1985 and was to receive the desert-pink ARTF scheme for Operation Granby in August 1990, although it did not participate in hostilities. It did, however, undertake UN peacekeeping operations and received the ARTF grey scheme in June 1993. Given the stage three modifications it remained with No. 6 Squadron and received a black tail as part of the Jaguars 25th-anniversary marks, although this had been removed by June 1999. Taken by road to St Athan on 21 February 2002 for upgrade to GR.3A it was returned to the squadron and in the disbandment reshuffle it was allocated the code 'EQ'. WFU at St Athan in March 2006, it was then sold to Everett Aerospace by August 2006 where it remained until June 2014 when it was sold to the Pima County Museum, Tucson, Arizona.

XZ397
S162 F/F 27 October 1977 (P. Ginger) in primer but wearing RAF serial. It undertook four production flights and was placed in store at Warton without being delivered to RAF. Identified for loan to India it was brought up to Jaguar International standard as G-27-322 with the F/F on 16 November 1979 and delivered to India as JI 006 on 11 December 1979. However, it crashed whilst in India on 14 June 1981 following a bird strike.

XZ398
S163 F/F 16 November 1977 (E. Bucklow) in primer wearing RAF serial and placed in store

at Warton but never delivered to the RAF. Identified for loan to India it was brought up to Jaguar International standard as G-27-323 and delivered to India as JI 007 on 14 August 1980. It was returned to the UK on 14 April 1984 and placed in short-term store again at Warton. It moved to JMU and was upgraded to GR.1A, being delivered to No. 6 Squadron as 'EF' on 7 February 1985. It was transferred to No. 41 Squadron as 'D' in August 1987 and then to No. 54 Squadron as 'GA' in June 1989. Following overhaul at the JMU in early 1991 it was returned to No. 41 Squadron as 'A', receiving the 75th-anniversary marking of red fin and spine and enlarged unit insignia. This was replaced by the ARTF grey scheme for overseas operations in June 1993 and then the new, permanent grey scheme, which was applied at St Athan in February 1996 with the jet adopting the two-letter code of 'FA'. Upgraded to GR.3 in December 1999 and then GR.3A in April 2004 it remained with the squadron until disbandment. It was then flown to RAF Cosford for ground instructional duties where it remains today.

XZ399

S164 F/F 23 November 1977 (E. Bucklow) and then placed in store at Warton. It was eventually delivered to RAF Coltishall on 17 May 1979 for the use of No. 6 Squadron. It operated during October 1980 with a white rectangle on the fin and upper-wing surfaces with the code 'EN'. Transferred to No. 14 Squadron as 'AG' on 10 January 1983, it was back with No. 6 Squadron as 'EL' on 9 February 1984 following attention at the JMU. It was then transferred to No. 226 OCU as code '09' by May 1984, then, following upgrade to GR.1A at the JMU in October 1985, it returned to No. 6

Squadron as 'EN'. Dispatched back to No. 226 OCU as '03' on 12 October 1987 it returned to No. 6 Squadron again as 'EJ' by June 1993 and became the Jaguar 97 trials aircraft in February 1999, and then as a GR.3A when under overhaul at St Athan in November 2000. The jet remained in service with No. 6 Squadron as code 'EJ' until disbandment. It undertook its last flight on 12 June 2007 to RAF Cosford for instructional duties.

XZ400

S165 F/F 16 February 1978 (E. Bucklow) and placed in store at Warton until undertaking a re-flight on production clearance on 12 March 1979 for development flying. D/D to RAF Coltishall on 29 June 1979 for use by No. 54 Squadron. Assigned code 'GP' it spent a short period in store at RAF Abingdon and then became the second aircraft to receive the avionics upgrade. Returned to No. 54 Squadron as a GR.1A on 9 December 1983 it was then damaged in a landing accident at RAF Honington on 7 February 1984 with the nose wheel partly retracted. Retained by No. 54 Squadron it had been recoded 'GH' by April 1986 and then transferred to No. 6 Squadron where it became 'EG'. Flown to RAF Shawbury for storage in June 1992, it remained there until overhaul beckoned at St Athan in March 1997, emerging in the new grey colour scheme when it returned to No. 54 Squadron as 'GR'. Upgraded to GR.3 at St Athan in May 2000 it was then dispatched to Warton to participate in the RR/Adour 106 engine upgrade trials. It returned to RAF Coltishall on 24 January 2002 as the first production aircraft, (of sixty-one planned) with the upgraded engine. Transferred to No. 41 Squadron as 'FQ' at the disbandment reshuffle it was flown to

St Athan on 6 July 2005 where it was WFU. It was sold to Everett Aerospace and delivered to the former RAF Bentwaters where it was last noted in July 2013.

ZB615

B38 F/F 23 September 1982 (Aitken / Hurst) as a T.2A and delivered to No. 5 MU RAF Kemble on 16 November 1982 for repainting into the RAE red, white and blue corporate colour scheme. The jet was initially assigned to the RAE at Farnborough then the DTEO-FJTS and ETPS. It was retired from use in November 2005.

N.B. None of this chapter comes from official sources and I am indebted to *British Aviation Review* and *Military Aircraft Review* for much of the information within this section.

The final Jaguar for UK use to be built at BAE Systems at Warton was ZB615. It undertook its first flight on 23 September 1982 and was delivered initially to No. 5MU at RAF Kemble on 16 November before onward delivery to Boscombe Down the following year, serving with the DTEO-FJTS/ETPS until it retired in November 2005.

GLOSSARY

A/C	Aircraft	JRRP	Jaguar Replacement Reconnaissance Pod
A&AEE	Aeroplane & Armament Experimental Establishment	L/F	Last Flight
AC	Air Co-operation	LRMTS	Laser Ranger and Marked Target Seeker
ARTF	Alkali Removable Temporary Finish	MoD	Ministry of Defence
ASTE	Aircraft & Systems Testing Establishment	MU	Maintenance Unit
ATC	Air Training Corps	NAF	Nigerian Air Force
BDRT	Battle Damage Repair Training	NATO	North Atlantic Treaty Organisation
COMED	Combined Map & Electronic Display	NAVWASS	Navigation and Weapon Aiming Sub-System
CTTO	Central Trials & Test Organisation	NWD	Nose Wheel Door
DARA	Defence Aviation Repair Agency	OCU	Operational Conversion Unit
DARIN	Display Attack and Ranging Inertial Navigation	OSD	Out of Service Date
D/D	Date Delivered	RAE	Royal Aircraft Establishment
DERA	Defence Evaluation & Research Agency	RAF	Royal Air Force
DRA	Defence Research Agency	RAFO	Royal Air Force of Oman
DSAT	Defence System Approach to Training	RFC	Royal Flying Corps
DTEO	Defence Test & Evaluation Organisation	SAM	Surface-to-Air Missile
ECM	Electronic Countermeasure	SAOEU	Strike Attack Operational Evaluation Unit
ETPS	Empire Test Pilots' School	SBAC	Society of British Aerospace Companies
F/F	First Flight	SOAF	Sultan of Oman Air Force
FAE	Fuerza Aérea Ecuatoriana	SoTT	School of Technical Training
FJ&WOEU	Fast Jet & Weapon Operational Evaluation Unit	Sqn	Squadron
FJTS	Fast Jet Test Squadron	TIALD	Thermal Imaging Airborne Laser Designation
FOC	Full Operating Clearance	TIRRS	Tornado Infrared Reconnaissance System
HUDWAC	Head-Up Display & Weapon Aiming Computer	TT	Total Time
IAF	Indian Air Force	TL	Total Landings
IOC	Initial Operating Clearance	UN	United Nations
ITP	Intent to Proceed	W/O	Written Off
JMU	Jaguar Maintenance Unit	WFU	Withdrawn From Use

Opposite: No. 6 Squadron undertake the final break at their farewell to Jaguar disbandment ceremony.

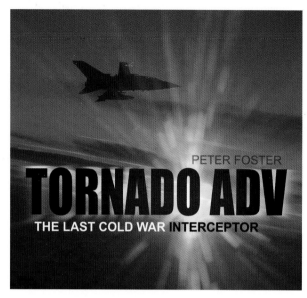

9780 7524 5936 3

Featuring complete histories of all stations and
squadrons to operate this type of aircraft alongside
individual airframe histories and stunningly illustrated
with a number of striking colour photographs, this
book charts the lifetime of a special aircraft forming a
perfect tribute to the Tornado ADV.

The destination for history
www.thehistorypress.co.uk